The Once and
Future Scriptures

The Once and Future Scriptures

Exploring the Role of the Bible in the Contemporary Church

Edited by
Gregory C. Jenks

Preface by Archbishop Phillip Aspinall

POLEBRIDGE PRESS
Salem, Oregon

This book is dedicated to our students at
St Francis Theological College in Brisbane.

Together we strive for the faith of the gospel.
συναθλοῦντες τῇ πίστει τοῦ εὐαγγελίου
—Phil 1:27

Cover and interior design by Robaire Ream

ISBN 978-1-59815-120-6

Table of Contents

Foreword

Few Anglicans in Brisbane have any depth of knowledge of the Bible; few read or study the Bible regularly; and few have any sense of encountering the reality of God in and through scripture. Consequently, few Anglicans speak passionately about their experience of God or feel comfortable speaking about their faith with others.

These shocking discoveries have been made in the Diocese of Brisbane over the last three years or so. Around half of the 140 parishes in the diocese have been participating in a project to reflect on and improve congregational health. And these outcomes about how Anglicans engage or not with Scripture have brought us up short.

Along with Mary, on the Feast of the Annunciation, I find myself asking, "How can this be?" The Bible is the bedrock of the faith. For two millennia it has inspired and sustained Christian people. It has been their weekly, even daily, diet. From its pages people have learned how to interpret and understand the world around them, how to make sense of history and how to discern right and wrong. How can it be that the significance and power of the Bible has waned to this extent, especially among people of faith?

A little knowledge and reflection identifies substantial reasons. The Enlightenment and the rise of modern science raised a host of questions about the presuppositions behind biblical stories. If the assumptions on which the stories are based no longer hold, can the stories themselves still be regarded as conveying truth? The advent of biblical criticism in the nineteenth century shook the foundations again. Applying the methods of historical and literary criticism to the Bible and setting aside a priori notions of sacredness and authority, in other words treating the Bible just like any other book, revealed its very human and fallible composition.

An intelligent reading of the Bible gives rise to all sorts of difficult questions for today's reader. Are they rendered relics of a bygone age, interesting ancient specimens, but devoid of contemporary meaning and power? Do they have any application in today's world? Do they have any truth to tell?

The Anglican Church itself, both in Australia and all over the world-wide Anglican Communion, has been riddled with conflict throughout living memory. Much of this has been closely related to how Scripture is interpreted and applied. In the 1960s and '70s arguments raged about the permissibility of remarrying divorced people in church. In the seventies, eighties and nineties debate raged over whether women could be ordained leaders in the church. Extending into the present, after decades of research and conflict, are questions about the rightful place of homosexual people in the life of the church, and particularly whether those in active gay relationships may be ordained or have their relationships blessed by the church. Temperatures still run high over all these issues, and they do not seem to lend themselves to clear-cut answers. Exactly what does Scripture teach or permit on these and other questions? And how can we responsibly arrive at answers?

Perhaps the ordinary members of the church have been exhausted by the seemingly endless debates or have tired of the difficulty in arriving at definitive, persuasive answers. And if they have given up on the church ever coming to a common mind, have they given up on the Bible too?

What are we to make today of the traditional understandings of the inspiration of Scripture, of the perspicuity of Scripture, of revelation, given what we now know about the human composition of the Bible? We can't unthink what scholarship has discovered. We know what we know. We cannot put the genie back in

the bottle, as author Peter Catt says in chapter 7, and go back to a time of peace untroubled by these questions.

But how should we move forward? Is it possible for today's Anglicans to hear God speaking through Scripture? After all, the whole point of listening to the Bible is to hear God speak. Is it possible in this day and age, knowing all that the Enlightenment, science and biblical criticism have discovered, to read and hear the Bible intelligently and to hear through Scripture the voice of God?

Resoundingly, yes! God still speaks to us and acts in the world as the Bible is read and heard and lived. We must approach Scripture, though, with alert and intelligent minds, not afraid to bring before it our heartfelt questions and to name our honest convictions. We must approach Scripture informed by the best scholarship on offer and in dialogue with everything other fields of endeavour have discovered of the truth. In the messiness and complexity and flawed character of these ancient texts we can hear afresh in their deepest trajectories, the voice of God calling us into life.

This collection of essays by Brisbane Anglican scholars, pastors and teachers is just such an honest grappling with heartfelt questions and honest convictions. Their wrestling leads us deeper into both our treasured heritage and the future which God's Word is still creating. We are indebted to them. And there is no better way to express our gratitude than to join them on that journey and to participate ourselves in that grappling. In precisely this way Anglicans can find in the Bible meaning, wisdom and power for living in the twenty-first century, and hear afresh the voice of God.

Phillip Aspinall
Archbishop of Brisbane
Primate, Anglican Church of Australia
Feast of the Annunciation, 2012

Contributors

Phillip Aspinall is Archbishop of Brisbane and Primate of the Anglican Church of Australia.

Gregory Jenks is a Senior Lecturer in the School of Theology at Charles Sturt University and Academic Dean of St Francis Theological College, Brisbane; Co-Director of the Bethsaida Excavations Project, Israel; and a Fellow of the Westar Institute, Willamette University. His publications include *The Once and Future Bible: An Introduction to the Bible for Religious Progressives* (2011) and *The Origins and Early Development of the Antichrist Myth* (1991).

Peter Catt is Dean of St John's Anglican Cathedral, Brisbane. Peter has degrees in Science and Theology. While Dean of Grafton Cathedral he established the International Festival of Philosophy, Science and Theology.

Susan Crothers-Robertson is Director of Formation at St Francis Theological College, Brisbane. Her doctoral research is investigating models of ministry formation within the Anglican communion that are responsive to the realities of current and future church contexts.

Marian Free has a PhD in New Testament from the University of Queensland, and is an Adjunct Lecturer in the School of Theology at Charles Sturt University. She teaches classes in New Testament and Christian Worship at St Francis Theological College. Marian is a Canon of St John's Cathedral, Brisbane, and Rector of St Augustine's Parish, Hamilton in Brisbane.

Nigel Leaves is Canon of St John's Anglican Cathedral, Brisbane and an Adjunct Lecturer in the School of Theology at Charles

Sturt University. He teaches undergraduate and postgraduate classes in Theology at St Francis Theological College. His publications include *Religion Under Attack: Getting Theology Right!* (2011), *The God Problem: Alternatives to Fundamentalism* (2006), *Surfing on the Sea of Faith: The Religion and Ethics of Don Cupitt* (2005), and *Odyssey on the Sea of Faith: The Life and Writings of Don Cupitt* (2004).

Steven Ogden is Principal of St Francis Theological College, Brisbane, and an Adjunct Lecturer in the School of Theology at Charles Sturt University. He was formerly Dean of St Peter's Cathedral, Adelaide. He is author of *Love Upside Down: Life, Love and the Subversive Jesus* (2011), *I Met God in Bermuda: Faith in the Twenty-First Century* (2009), and *The Presence of God in the World* (2007).

Cathy Thomson has a PhD in Theology from Flinders University of South Australia, and is currently the Rector of Christ Church, St Lucia in Brisbane. A member of the Anglican-Lutheran International Commission, Cathy is an Adjunct Lecturer in the School of Theology at Charles Sturt University and teaches Theology at St Francis Theological College. She is co-editor of *Ordination of Women: Interdenominational Perspectives* (2006, with Victor C. Pfitzner), a contributor to *Faithfulness in Fellowship* (2001), and co-editor of *Faithfulness in Fellowship: A Study Guide* (2003, with Muriel Porter).

Abbreviations

Exod	Exodus
Isa	Isaiah
Hos	Hosea
Matt	Matthew
Rom	Romans
Gal	Galatians
Phil	Philippians
Col	Colossians
Heb	Hebrews
LXX	The ancient Greek versions of the Bible, commonly known as the Septuagint
MT	Masoretic Text
NT	New Testament
NRSV	New Revised Standard Version
OT	Old Testament

Introduction

Gregory C. Jenks

Theology in general, and biblical studies in particular, are inherently public and collective activities. They derive from and exist for those communities of religious practice that we know as churches, communions, denominations, movements, religions, and sects. Yet, as a contemporary academic discipline, theology tends to be an individual pursuit. Unlike the sciences, in which a great deal of research is collaborative, drawing on the shared resources of a research team, theology is often undertaken by scholars working in isolation as they prepare their best ideas for anonymous peer review, and then defend their published work from criticism.

The tendency to fragmentation and isolation within theological scholarship is also seen in the lack of collaboration across the internal disciplinary boundaries. Biblical scholars, historians, and theologians too often communicate only within our own sub-disciplines. Our students bravely do their best to connect the dots and bring their biblical scholarship into dialogue with their theology studies. Our graduates in pastoral ministry despair of keeping up, and famously revert to attitudes and practices acquired before entering the seminary. Meanwhile the church limps on.

Each time we distance ourselves from a historical or theological claim in the Bible that we no longer find credible, the authority of the Scriptures is eroded. In our natural reluctance to revise our traditional formularies that describe the Bible as the 'word of God', we may be consigning the Bible to irrelevance. On the other hand, critical religion scholarship—and other far-reaching changes in our understanding of ourselves as humans and of the web of life of which we are integral elements—offers us the opportunity to re-imagine the Bible, taking it seriously while

1

refusing to take it literally. In the process of being honest with each other about the historical, literary and religious character of the Bible, we also have an opportunity to re-affirm our belief that God is encountered when these sacred texts are read from the vantage point of faith, hope, and love.

In this book, the academic theologians have emerged from our studies to engage in a public conversation about the kind of Bible we have and some ways in which we might draw on those Scriptures for the sake of critical, robust theology in the service of the church. This is not a book of answers, but it is a dialogue between scholars who are also people of faith. In this dialogue we find that the Bible is not only a 'problem' for the church, but also a source of faith, hope, and deep wisdom.

You are invited to join the conversation. We hope you will come with us on the journey, which is both an adventure and a pilgrimage. We travel as people of faith, and among our most treasured possessions are these ancient writings that constitute the Christian Bible. We are not the only travellers on this road, and the Bible is not the only sacred text that serves to shape the holy imagination of our fellow pilgrims. But we are Christians, and more specifically Anglicans with a deep love of our church's ancient traditions, forms of ministry, sacraments, and—in particular—the Scriptures that have such a special place in the life of our church.

This book has been written in part as a theological response to *The Once and Future Bible*, in which I provided an introduction to the Bible for religious progressives. That book offers an overview of both the contents of the Bible and contemporary biblical scholarship. Necessarily, it left open a number of important questions about the implications of such an understanding of the Bible for Christian belief and practice in our own times.

In this volume, I am joined by a number of colleagues from St Francis Theological College in Brisbane, as we explore some of those implications. Peter Catt, Dean of St John's Cathedral in Brisbane and a colleague in the ministry formation programs of the College, has joined our conversation and brings his particular expertise in the dialogue between science and religion to our circle.

We are honoured that the Most Reverend Dr Phillip Aspinall, Archbishop of Brisbane and Primate of the Anglican Church of Australia, has contributed a Foreword. This does not imply his agreement with the essays in this book, but it is a tangible expression of the importance of such thoughtful conversations about the Bible for the future and for the wellbeing of the church in the twenty-first century.

In the first essay, I outline briefly how critical biblical scholarship has made traditional affirmations about the Bible problematic. As a case study—relevant to our own context as contributors but also more widely among the Christian churches—I discuss the challenges flowing from the special place ascribed to the Bible within the Anglican Church of Australia.

Cathy Thomson ("Scripture as Normative Source in Theology") addresses the issue of God's presence in the processes of our engagement with Scripture. She offers us the evocative formula of the Bible's "human (yet graced) composition" combined with the "holy susceptibility of the reader." Before considering the specific case of how the early church came to develop its teachings about Jesus as 'son of God' and as 'divine', she notes a number of ethical constraints which bear on the process of interpretation of Scripture and from which she derives five principles that may be helpful in guiding our use of Scripture as a 'source' in theology.

In chapter three, "Wisdom as Well as Facts", Steven Ogden addresses the polemic between fundamentalists and progressives over the authority of Scripture. His concern with this conflict is that it is an unwinnable war. Fundamentalism, by definition, is not interested in an open conversation. In contrast, the progressive movement is committed to a process of dialogue. While it has a lot to offer, its approach to biblical interpretation is constrained by a narrow view of history, epistemology and human experience. In particular, progressive theology simplifies the discipline of history and overestimates the value of its contribution. In this light, Steven makes a plea for the epistemological value of experience in interpreting sacred texts; that is, a story like the Parable of the Lost Son has significance because it rings true.

In "Scripture, God-Talk and Jesus", Nigel Leaves differs from Steven Ogden over the impossibility of beginning with historical information when constructing theology. Nigel argues that to be *distinctively* Christian discourse about God, theology must begin with the historical Jesus and seek to trace the glimpses of God's reality observed in Jesus' words and actions as set out in the Scriptures. This is no abstract academic exercise, but fundamental to understanding the God that is to be proclaimed by the Church today. The future of Christianity depends on theology that is inclusive and non-dogmatic, which was what Jesus taught. In short, to have seen Jesus is to have seen God!

Susan Crothers-Robertson ("Scripture and Formation for Ministry") considers the role of Scripture in forming candidates for ordained ministry. Susan takes issue with J. I. Packer's view that candidates and their future parishes are not well-served by an exposure to critical biblical scholarship. Citing the classic prayer for grace to "hear . . . read, mark, learn and inwardly digest" the Scriptures, she explores the many different ways that the Scriptures impact the ministry formation of ordination candidates.

One of the most influential contexts for Scripture in the life of the church is found in the liturgies of the gathered communities. For many people this is the only, or at least their most significant, encounter with Scripture. In "The Bible and Liturgy", Marian Free considers different dimensions of the way Scripture operates in public worship: as liturgical texts, as shared story from which we derive identity, as lectionary, and as preached word. Marian encourages us to embrace critical scholarship and not lose our nerve as we fashion the future of today's church.

Peter Catt contributes the final essay, "Scripture, Science and the Big Story". He invites us to look beyond what he calls the 'Christian metanarrative' to the new grand story that is taking hold of the public imagination. As the current use of the biblical narrative proves itself increasingly irrelevant to the global society of the post-Christian era, Peter suggests that narrative theology offers a way for Christians to engage with—and contribute to—the emerging 'big story'. He particularly appreciates the work of Pierre Teilhard de Chardin as a demonstration of the capacity for the Christian story to engage creatively with our new knowledge of cosmos and psyche.

The essays that comprise this book are offered as a contribution to the necessary conversation about how Australian Anglicans might best understand our own reception of the Bible. At the same time, and perhaps *because* of their particularity in the context of our own church, these essays may be of value to Australian Christians from other traditions, to Anglicans in other parts of the world, and also to Christians of many different traditions in various parts of the world.

1

The 'Problem' of the Bible

Gregory C. Jenks

> When Christians speak of the Bible as 'inspired', . . . [this] is an inchoate way of saying that the entire traditioning process continues and embodies a surplus rendering of reality that discloses all of reality in the light of the holiness of YHWH. Through that disclosure that happens in fits and starts through human imagination and human ideology—but is not finally domesticated by either human imagination or human ideology—we receive a 'revelation' of the hiddenness of the life of the world and of God's life in the world. And because we in the church find it so, we dare to say in the actual traditioning process with trembling lips, 'The Word of the Lord . . . Thanks be to God.'
> —Walter Brueggemann[1]

The carefully crafted words cited above reflect a key concern with which each and every essay in this book is engaged, including this opening contribution. For people of Christian faith, the Bible is both a sacred text and a sacred site, a place where we encounter the Spirit of God. The special and sacred character of the Scriptures has too often seduced believers into making unjustifiable claims on behalf of these special writings, and yet even to claim an encounter with God in these texts is itself a complex and inchoate statement of faith. Brueggemann is evocative when he describes the tentative ("with trembling lips") dimensions of acknowledging and affirming the ways that Scripture can be received as 'word of the Lord'.

As the opening contribution in this collection, the present chapter has the task of stating the other side of the same reality. For all that Scripture is received as 'word of the Lord', it is also a problematic text for theologians, for the churches, and for the everyday Christian. This chapter will identify and explore selected aspects of the problem posed by the Bible in our time and place, and will seek to set an agenda for subsequent contributions to address in their turn.

A Brief History of Reception

This is not the place to attempt a detailed description of how the Bible has been received and interpreted over almost two thousand years of Christian history.[2] However, it is timely to offer some observations that will provide context for the ensuing discussion.

While the emergence of the Bible was critical for the survival of Judaism and the development of Christianity, the Scriptures emerged within Christianity in historical circumstances that meant their form and function within the faith community was not a matter for explicit discussion. As has often been observed, Christianity was born with the Bible in the cradle and its continued presence was rarely a matter for debate.

The earliest Christians were observant Jews and possessed a traditional set of sacred writings. Their religious practices assigned considerable significance to the role of these sacred writings within a religious community that increasingly found itself in diaspora communities around the ancient world, or at least some distance from Jerusalem and its temple. Indeed, rather than pilgrimage to Jerusalem, the more literary processes of biblical interpretation were central to Christian mission and theology. Paul, for instance, urged his converts to learn from the sacred texts, but he did not encourage them to visit the temple.

Compared to Jews and Muslims, Christians have a very weak connection to place. We do not preserve a tradition of particular places as our primary location within the divine ordering of the cosmos. Our celebration of the sacraments is intrinsically timeless and placeless. This is sometimes stated in more positive terms as *eternal* and *universal*. Pilgrimage has rarely been a significant element in the larger practice of our religion, although it has been encouraged around the sites associated with particular saints and religious experiences. There is no Christian equivalent to the *hajj* as a key religious obligation.

Without a unique attachment to land and city, and with no central tradition of pilgrimage, Christianity is much more attached to the local community of faith as the sacred site for engagement with God and with fellow believers. Within that context, the Bible has a special role as a religious artefact shared with believers across multiple locations and over the generations. It is the quintessential mobile religious device for a community characterized from its beginnings by dispersion.

There seems to be have been no debate within earliest Christianity about the content, form or authority of the Scriptures inherited from Judaism. It is only with Marcionism— which flourished around 140 CE, and thus already represents a third or fourth generation of Christian practice—that we find controversy over the inclusion of these Jewish texts in the Christian Bible. As it happened, Marcion's radical program to eliminate Jewish elements in Christianity only served to reinforce the attachment of the wider Christian community to those texts.

The evidence of the ancient biblical manuscripts suggests a widespread practice of reading, copying and interpreting texts that are now familiar to us from the Western canon of the Bible along with many texts that are unfamiliar to us. These less familiar texts have been excluded from the canon, or relegated to deuterocanonical status, as a result of various internal religious controversies over the centuries. The struggle between Catholic Christianity and Gnostic Christianity resulted in a preference for

New Testament (NT) writings with an apparent apostolic connection, while the Protestant Reformation in the fifteenth and sixteenth centuries resulted in the elimination of books found only in the Greek version of the Old Testament.

The surprising informality of this whole process is reflected in the definition of canonical boundaries in the *Articles of Religion* for the Church of England at the time of the Reformation:

> In the name of the Holy Scripture we do understand those canonical Books of the Old and New Testament, of whose authority was never any doubt in the Church. . . . And the other Books (as Hierome saith) the Church doth read for example of life and instruction of manners; but yet doth it not apply them to establish any doctrine. . . . All the Books of the New Testament, as they are commonly received, we do receive, and account them Canonical. (Article 6)

This portion of the article appeals to a general reception of the biblical books. Anglicans were to accept those books "of whose authority was never any doubt". The specific New Testament books did not even need to be listed, but simply described as those "commonly received". There was no attempt either to invoke any authoritative ancient decision or to make such a formal declaration as a national church.

Throughout the first fifteen hundred years of Christianity the Bible was primarily a text for the religious professionals, rather than a resource for the spiritual edification of the common Christian. Due to the constraints of technology and literacy levels, few ordinary Christians would ever have seen a Bible, much less owned a copy. Rather, clergy and lay members of religious orders would have been familiar with anthologies of biblical material prepared for particular liturgical contexts: breviaries, gospel books, and psalters. Not surprisingly, lectionaries are the most common form of biblical manuscripts available to scholars as we trace the history of the Bible and its reception in Christianity.

In the Western Church, the Bible was reinvented as a tool for shaping the life of the Church and the pious individual at the time of the Reformation. This was mostly due to the particular history of the Protestant dispute with Rome, but it was only possible due to the invention of the printing press and the increase in literacy levels outside the religious work force. The pious Christian could now possess and study the Bible for himself (sic), and the power of Pope and Church to control the religious imagination of the West was in terminal decline.

Since the Reformation, grassroots Christian views of the Bible have become increasingly exaggerated and naïve, claiming far too much for the Bible. In this uncritical attachment to the Bible (known as 'Biblicism') the Christian Scriptures are defended as uniquely authoritative, inerrant, infallible, historically correct, self-sufficient, internally consistent, self-evident in their meaning, and universally applicable.[3]

The cultural revolution of the Enlightenment would soon mean that this high-water mark of the Bible's influence in Christian practice would subside as the Bible became the site for a profound and continuing challenge to the authority of the church. For cultural, historical, political, and social reasons, the nature and authority of the Scriptures were challenged by humanists and defended by religionists. The controversy continues to our own time, although the churches mostly act as if the authority of the Bible is beyond question. In formal religious statements it often remains sufficient simply to cite a biblical reference to settle a theological point.

In the contemporary church we can observe both conservative and progressive readings of Scriptures. This is a divide that cuts across traditional Catholic/Protestant, Conservative/ Liberal categories, and it exposes a reactionary/progressive dynamic within all expressions of Christianity. As people of faith, do we read Scripture primarily to preserve and protect beliefs, rituals and roles inherited from the past, or to seek new insights and gain fresh wisdom for the challenges of being faithful today? And, if both, then what kind of creative balance is achieved, and how is it maintained?

At the heart of critical biblical scholarship—and indeed all scholarship, religious or otherwise—is a critical mindset that challenges traditional ways of thinking, including time-honoured ways of using Scripture. The critical method is a sustained existential interrogative: Why? Why that? Why now? Why here? Why not? What if?

One significant danger associated with such a sustained critical perspective is the risk of discarding too much wisdom from the past in the quest for new and improved solutions to current challenges. But that risk does not outweigh the advantages of fresh insights that may arise from a persistent quest for improvement: better analysis, better diagnosis, and better praxis.

While critical religion scholarship has its own philosophical and theological grounds for such a critical (prophetic?) stance towards the tradition, it also acts as part of a broad progressive cultural alliance. While ascendant religion tends to cling to power and protect its privileges, prophetic religion operates from the margins of respectability and may find common ground with artists, philosophers, scientists, and literary scholars.

Points of Confrontation and Challenge

We can usefully consider the problem posed by the Bible for theologians and church leaders under three categories: the world *behind* the text, the world *within* the text, and the world *before* the text. This metaphor of three biblical 'worlds' has been developed by Sandra Schneiders,[4] and it will allow us to group the major problematic dimensions of the Bible according to their primary location in the historical world behind the text, within the text itself, or within our own acts of interpretation as readers.

The World behind the Biblical Text

From the perspective of the world behind the biblical text, a considerable number of challenges are posed for people of faith by critical biblical scholarship. The central characteristic of these challenges relates to the deconstructive impact of critical attention to questions of historicity, to traditional assumptions about the origins of the biblical writings, and to the increased number of ancient manuscripts now available to scholars.

As a result of our increased knowledge of the ancient past, the historical character of the Bible has been seriously compromised. The relationship between what 'actually happened' in the ancient past and how those events are narrated in the biblical texts is far more complex than has often been assumed by previous generations of Bible readers. At the same time as the historicity of the Bible has been challenged, we have been able to gain a much more accurate understanding of the cultural and social dynamics of the ancient communities who first created and used these texts. We find ourselves knowing more about what life was like 'back then', and yet also being less certain of the historicity of the biblical narratives. In this complex process it is tempting to seek short-term polemical advantage in certain discoveries or models but perhaps wiser to refrain from doing so.

The need to suspend judgment on the historicity of the biblical narrative already implies a significant reduction of the claims so often made on behalf of the Bible and its contribution to Christian thought and practice. While it seems certain that 'David' was a ruler in Jerusalem during the tenth century BCE, it is even more certain that his achievements were nothing like those attributed to him in the Bible, and his vast empire is an exercise in religious imagination. Such historical reservations have significant religious and theological implications for people for whom God's 'mighty acts' in the past are the basis of faith here and now. What if those mighty acts are fictional?

Not only are the events represented in the Bible more often fictional than historical, but the texts themselves have an uncertain pedigree as well as a confused history of copying and transmission. Moses did not write the Pentateuch, and David did not write the Psalms. More seriously, the Dead Sea Scrolls demonstrate that only Psalms 1–91 were finalized by the second century BCE, and that books such as Samuel and Jeremiah existed in both longer and shorter versions just a century or so before the time of Jesus.

Critical investigation of the world behind the biblical texts has established beyond reasonable doubt that the origins of the Bible were very different than Christians like to imagine. While this does not prevent us using the Scriptures in new and creative ways, it does require us to rethink how these sacred texts function in the life of the contemporary church.

The World within the Biblical Text

As questions around the world behind the text multiplied, some scholars turned their attention to the world within the biblical text. Here we seem to be on firmer ground. No longer adrift in a world of historical ambiguity, the reader can simply engage with the texts as they stand. The historical questions can be set aside as we enter the world of the text.

In this hermeneutical move, the focus shifts from defending the historicity of the Bible to appreciating the literary artistry of the authors. But these were human authors, and ancient ones, as well. They imagined their texts under the influence of literary and rhetorical conventions that are very different from those of today's readers. These writers were shaped by Homer, and operated on the basis of mimesis and intertextual dynamics whose finer points escape us moderns.

The nagging historical anxiety of the modern West refuses to leave us alone even in the relative sanctuary of the biblical text. Are we reading accounts of actual events or symbolic narratives?

And even when the events may have happened (as with the crucifixion of Jesus), is the narrative more the product of imagination
than memory? Is everything just melting away into (mere) story?
Does this wonderful narrative have any basis in real events in the
lives of actual people? Is Christian faith anything more than a
heroic act of imagination?

More confrontational still, what of the unacceptable values
and immoral practices encoded in the text?[5] Even if God did not
command the ethnic cleansing of ancient Palestine, the Bible
seems to have been written and approved by people who liked to
imagine that God did. These sacred texts are increasingly recognized as artefacts created by persons with particular cultural and
religious agendas in the ancient world, and the modern reader
can find herself an intruder in an unfamiliar landscape when exploring the world of the text.

The World before the Text

Then there is the world before the text, the lived realities of the
actual readers here and now. Not only is it clear that it makes a
difference *who* is doing the reading, it is also becoming increasingly clear that a text without a reader is a document that has no
significance.

The impact of different readers is simple enough to recognize.
Not only do different people discover (construct?) different
meanings in the same text, but the same persons at different
times in their own practice as readers will report finding quite
different meanings in the same texts. It is for this reason, surely,
that a classic text such as the Twenty-third Psalm can be read at
funerals as well as at weddings. The text has not changed, but
the readers and their contexts certainly have.

As scholars of communication and literature rethink the
relationship between author, text and reader there are clear
implications for Scripture, which exists and functions as text at
the hands and in the imaginations of readers. We are learning to

reimagine what a text is and how it operates. While every text comes with certain assumptions, those operating conditions may not be valid at the time when it is read.

To remain significant, and especially to continue as a site for divine-human encounter, the Bible may need to be read contrary to its literal and historical significance. Only then can it serve as a source of wisdom for readers in contexts beyond the imagination of its authors and previous readers. This is a necessary corollary for a sacred text in a religious tradition that accords primacy to the freedom of the divine Spirit to speak a prophetic word to the contemporary context of the faithful. However, it destabilizes both the text and the traditional interpretations of its significance. Under what conditions could we ever imagine the Bible to be the unchanging and self-explicating revelation of what the Spirit is saying to the churches?

As contemporary readers of Scripture, we are alert to the impact of unequal distributions of power—within and beyond the community of faith. We are alert to the multivalent significance of the text to readers of particular ethnicity, gender, sexuality and status. We note the abuse of creation implicit in many biblical texts and much Christian theology, and we acknowledge the power of prior commitments to filter the meanings we discover in Scripture.

As we seek to engage faithfully with the God to whom the Scriptures bear witness, we may also come to appreciate that 'faith' is an attitude of vulnerable trust generated and practiced in the here and now, rather than derived from either the actual events that may have happened once upon a time or the literary qualities of the text. What matters most to me now is not whether Abraham and Sarah trusted YHWH, but whether I am going to spend my allocated span of human existence in an act of trust akin to that of Jesus. What does it mean for me to be a person of faith here and now? How is that shaped and informed by the Bible? How little does the Bible really matter when the time comes for me to choose how to live faithfully right now, right here?

As residents of the global village, we are also inevitably aware of the problem posed by claims to unique truth. My village includes good people who do not share my religious outlook, and in many cases have their own traditional wisdom that seems to serve them well in the task of shaping lives that are holy and true. The village also includes scoundrels and villains, whose dark propensity for evil threatens both the well being of the village and the carefully nuanced optimism of my own decision to live as a person of faith. The mono-cultural assumptions of the Bible seem radically incompatible with the realities of life in the twenty-first century.

Implications for Theologians,
Churches and Believers

The first and most far-reaching implication for theologians, for churches, and for everyday people of faith, is that the Bible is simply not capable of sustaining all the demands made of it. The more we know about the Bible, the worlds from which it derives, and the dynamics of reading any text in our own time and place, the less the Bible is able to live up to our expectations. For its own sake as much as for ours, the role of the Bible needs to be re-imagined.

In our concern to defend, protect and retain the Bible we may too easily find ourselves engaging in a biblical version of the 'god-of-the-gaps' strategy. Rather than seeking to defend the Bible by protecting it from critical attention, we may do best to liberate the Bible from the unfortunate and unsustainable expectations of the religious. Neither the Bible nor God is well served by any tactics that seek to protect the Bible from scrutiny.

We must, therefore, resist any temptation to treat our sacred texts differently than the way we treat other people's sacred texts. Legend and self-serving fiction are to be found in the Bible just as surely as they are in the sacred traditions of other communities. Ancient texts, and indeed all written texts, are ambiguous preparations for an act of communication that will necessarily be driven and controlled by the reader (rather than the author). This dynamic needs to be embraced, not ignored. It cannot be obscured by an appeal to divine inspiration.

There is a kind of *kenotic* (self-limiting) principle that applies to the Bible as much as to Jesus. If God chooses to communicate with humanity through written documents, then that communication is necessarily constrained by the inherent dynamics of the process. The human origins of the texts, and the vulnerable circumstances of the Bible's preservation and transmission, will necessarily need to be taken into account. So will the complex processes of reading and interpretation through which a reader creates meaning. Even an inspired book requires a very ordinary human reader in order to have any meaning.

When it comes to the question of historicity—that 'Holy Grail' to which western culture has mortgaged so much of our concept of truth—we shall need to accept and work within the methodological constraints of critical historiography. As ancient oriental literature, the Bible comes from times and places that are profoundly foreign to us, and will forever remain strange; even when we delude ourselves into imagining that we are comprehending and practicing 'biblical values'. The biblical narratives may well preserve memories of ancient events and relationships, but their primary character is to proclaim the worldview (the faith and the practices) of ancient Jewish and Christian communities, not to address our misplaced obsession with history. They are sacred texts for us because of their religious value, not because of their historical worth.

Although we feel the loss that necessarily follows from such a decision, we shall need to embrace a methodological bias towards scepticism in our reading of our own sacred texts. Minimalist historical claims will be matched with modest theological claims,

in part as reparations for the past excesses of theological trium-
phalism. Better to take our place lower down the table and be
called up higher, than to overreach ourselves and be shamed into
a public confession of religious hubris.

The value of our religious traditions will not be their assumed
superiority over the traditions of other religious communities.
Nor will we make the mistake of thinking that the validity of
our tradition is derived from either its historicity or the capacity of earlier generations to express themselves in ways that we
moderns find cogent or convincing. Rather, the value of our
tradition—and ultimately of the Bible itself—will be generated
by the capacity of Christianity to facilitate human transformation
and ecological justice; taking us beyond ourselves for the sake of
the larger web of life at whose centre we find God.

The God celebrated and proclaimed by this kind of Christianity
will draw us beyond the Christian Scriptures, but we shall never
leave them behind. They will not need to be defended from
criticism, but neither will they be invoked as a simple recipe for
a successful life in the present time. Theologians, churches and
everyday believers will find ourselves drawn into fresh explora-
tions of truth in a quest for holy wisdom.

Such a process will be challenging, and even confronting, for
the churches. Not only will we need to learn how to read the
Bible differently, we shall need to rewrite so much of our creeds
and liturgies. Instead of rehearsing the mighty acts of God in
times past, we shall focus on discerning the wisdom of God for
the present times. Canonical boundaries will not vanish, but
their significance may once again decrease as the function of
Scripture changes from enforcing the boundaries of acceptability
to enlarging the boundaries of our spiritual imagination.

The Anglican Crisis over the Bible

My own context within the Anglican Church of Australia invites
me to understand our work in this volume within the larger

reality of the Anglican Communion and the more local dynamics of Australian Anglicanism.

Christians within the Anglican/Episcopalian tradition place great value on the Scriptures. These sacred writings do far more than serve as a source and reference point for our beliefs and behaviours. Our public liturgies that have such a defining role in constituting Anglican identity and practice are deeply indebted to the Bible. As Marian Free observes, the Scriptures provide a significant proportion of the words we share in worship (see chapter 6). At the same time, Anglicans have been 'early adopters' of the new critical approaches to Scripture. Anglicans value intellectual inquiry and are predisposed to integrate the insights of new knowledge into our faith and practice.

As much as any Christian community—and perhaps more so than some—Anglicans are struggling with questions of authority, identity, mission, and relevance. At the centre of these conflicts—found at both national and international levels of our life together—lies a set of unresolved questions over the nature of the Bible and its authority in the life of the church. We take the Scriptures seriously, yet may not feel obliged to take them literally.

This struggle over the Bible is particularly challenging for Australian Anglicans as the Constitution of our national church gives the Scriptures special authority on the basis of their "inspiration" by God:

> This Church receives all the canonical scriptures of the Old and New Testaments as being the ultimate rule and standard of faith given by inspiration of God and containing all things necessary for salvation.[6]

While the Constitution of our church has no particular spiritual or theological authority, it does provide the legal framework for our life together as a voluntary association within the larger Australian society. In a profound sense, reception of the Bible as an authoritative revelation from God is part of our covenant with one another as Anglicans in this country. For the sake of our shared life together we need to speak clearly and consistently about the Scriptures.

At first glance the declaration about the Bible (one of three such unalterable 'fundamental' statements at the beginning of the Constitution) seems simply to reiterate historic Reformation principles, but that is not quite the case. The affirmation that the Bible contains "all things necessary for salvation" is a restatement of one part only of the relevant material from article 6 of the *Articles of Religion.* It chooses to affirm the positive dimension of the article (Scripture contains all we need for salvation), but refrains from affirming the negative dimension of the same article:

> Holy Scripture containeth all things necessary to salvation: so that whatsoever is not read therein, nor may be proved thereby, is not to be required of any man, that it should be believed as an article of the Faith, or be thought requisite or necessary to salvation. In the name of the Holy Scripture we do understand those canonical Books of the Old and New Testament, of whose authority was never any doubt in the Church.

The opening clause of this fundamental declaration also reduces the more explicit statement of article 6. It simply refers to the "canonical scriptures of the Old and New Testament". In doing so, the Constitution begs the question of which books are "canonical". Given other references to the *Articles of Religion* in the Constitution, we may presume this is intended to relegate the Deuterocanonical books to a lesser status and promote the narrow Old Testament canon preferred by the Protestant reformers.

The most significant change to the view of Scripture that is embedded in the Constitution concerns the description of the relationship of God to the origins of the Bible. With its direct statement that the Scriptures are "given by inspiration of God", the Constitution seems to narrow the traditional description of that relationship, such as we find in the question addressed to candidates for ordination as Deacons in *A Prayer Book for Australia*:

> Do you wholeheartedly accept the canonical scriptures of the Old and New Testament, as given by the Spirit to convey in many and varied ways the revelation of God which is fulfilled in our Lord Jesus Christ? [AAPB, 786]

Needless to say, these are carefully crafted words. The care that went into their composition reflects both the significance of Scripture for the life of the Church, and the polemic around the nature and authority of the Bible in the contemporary Church.

What are we to make of the "many and varied ways" in which the Spirit conveys through the Scriptures the revelation of God that is fulfilled in Jesus? Are metaphorical and non-literal readings of Scriptures part of that diversity? How is the activity of the Spirit in the act of reading and receiving the Scriptures to be included in our understanding of the Bible? How do we account for the diversity of meaning derived from the same Scriptures?

The Ordinal reflects a more nuanced view of the nature and authority of Scripture, and of the relation of God to the text, than seems to have been in the mind of those drafting the Constitution. Yet neither the Ordinal nor the Constitution settles the matter for us.

The Constitution does not define precisely what "given by inspiration of God" might mean. At its weakest form, this could simply be an affirmation that the collection of books that now constitutes the Bible came to exist providentially as God directed ('inspired') the complex and very human processes of reception. In its strongest form, the phrase could be understood as affirming that the authors of the biblical documents wrote only those words that God wished them to record.

The continuing debates within both Australian Anglicanism and the international Anglican Communion indicate there is no consensus on what we mean when ascribing to God some role in the creation of the Bible. As the Bible itself is ambiguous over the matter, this confusion is not surprising. This confusion within the churches is compounded by the impact of critical biblical scholarship on the ways in which the Bible is now received by many people of faith. Can critical scholarship assist us to determine how broadly to interpret these ecclesial formulae?

For Australian Anglicans—even more sharply than for Christians of other traditions and Anglicans of other ecclesial provinces—the deconstructive impact of critical biblical scholarship is especially problematic. Individually and collectively we need to address the questions for Christian belief and practice that flow from the assumptions, methods, and outcomes of biblical criticism.

The essays that follow in this book offer thoughtful responses to this 'problem' of the Bible for the contemporary church. In their own ways, these essays are examples of that nuanced appreciation of Scripture described by Walter Brueggemann in his words quoted at the beginning of this chapter. While acknowledging the complexities of human imagination and human ideology that have produced these sacred writings, with trembling lips—and as part of an on-going and Spirit-breathed traditioning process—we acknowledge them as 'word of the Lord'. Thanks be to God.

Notes

1. *Introduction to the Old Testament*, 10–11.

2. For a brief discussion of these issues, and for suggestions for further reading, see "The Use and Abuse of the Bible" in Jenks, *The Once and Future Bible*, especially pp. 18–23.

3. For a recent critique of Biblicism from an Evangelical perspective see Smith, *The Bible Made Impossible*.

4. Schneiders, *The Revelatory Text*. For a discussion of hermeneutical methods relevant to these three 'worlds', see Jenks, *The Once and Future Bible*, 38–50.

5. Note the recent collection of essays around the question of 'animosity' in the Bible: Fitzgerald et al., *Animosity, the Bible, and Us*.

6. http://www.anglican.org.au/docs/ACAConstitution-2003.pdf.

2

Scripture as Normative Source in Theology

Cathy Thomson

Fore-"word"

Today within a postmodern thought and language milieu, you have to be really careful about words. Arguably, every essay should begin at the very least with attempted definition of the words of the title. Thus, theology begins somewhat improbably in semiology. Here, when the little that can be said to be securely 'denoted' is ascertained, there emerges the poetic subversion that is connotation, at once powerfully suggestive and poignantly insecure. Of course, it has always been so. Language whispers meaning as the merest breath of air, and meaning is borne in the unevenness of surface inscription or the fragility of disconnected sound. The suggestion that there is 'non-correspondence' between a word, a sign or a symbol, and its meaning is best understood with reference to the work of Ferdinand de Saussure and Jacques Derrida; Saussure through the concept of 'arbitrariness', Derrida through the notion of *différence*.[1]

Scripture

The theological corollary of such 'language games'[2] is the suggestion that divinity might somehow be recollected in the frailty of human flesh, that the eternal might be discerned in the temporal. The Christian tradition recognizes and asserts at its heart the unfathomable mystery of Incarnation, and this is something that pertains to Holy Scripture, too. Scripture provides temporal expression of the eternal, through human witnesses reflecting on their experience of God, and that of their communities. The risk is that all that might be claimed in the intercourse between author and reader is that a sensibility was grasped or even (heaven of heaven) shared. Enough of these 'aha!' moments,[3] and them shared, and we have the delicate but recognizable beginnings of a filmy fabric of belief.

Scripture—that (sacred) book—has sacred possibility only through its human (yet graced) composition and compilation, and the holy susceptibility of the reader. This realization, however, suggests an ethical constraint barring claims to too much truth. We might not like it, but there it is. It is with the blessed constraint of anticipating no possibility (of absolute truth) and every possibility (of God's grace), and these at one and the same time that I, the theologian, take Holy Scripture into my hands. What sort of theologian? One formed only in the warp and weft, in the matrix of interpretative (and graced) possibility. The reader-theologian actualizes meaning "in, with and under"[4] the words of Scripture; and is actualized by them. It is a risky business, but it is also blessed. For does not God the Holy Spirit with the angels and archangels and the whole company of heaven—not to mention the "raggle taggle gypsies-o"[5] of the church militant here on earth—attend every tentative transaction?

Normative

We have begun to explore the 'Scripture' of the title. Let us now barter the coin of 'normativity'. Normativity is claimed by those who wish to establish a norm. Does Scripture establish a norm, or even a set of norms? What, all of it? . . . and the *same* norm(s)? Rowan Williams acknowledges that through literary theory "we have been taught a certain uneasiness about the whole notion of normative meaning".[6] Clearly the impulse to lay claim to normativity as a function of the content of a text is stretched and 'rattled' beyond credibility. Perhaps we might be helped by an exploration of what is usual within a 'normativity' thought-framework. What is often found here are standards, patterns, types, or customs to govern a set of practices or behaviours. One emerging insight is therefore that normativity is usually about the management or control of behaviour(s). Within a faith community this might of course, and validly, be referred to as 'guidance' rather than control. So it is not so much that these paltry reflections of mine are intended to usurp entirely the concept of normativity, but that they begin to suggest that caution ought to be exercised against the making of exorbitant moral claims about any posited 'norm'.

Source

Ahh . . . observe . . . this normativity is the normativity of the 'source'. The theological reader loves the quest for the source. The source is theological 'grist for the mill'! Yet, maddeningly, within the very theological discipline that reveres it, the search for the source is an almost fallacious proposition. The source is the word spoken; the spirit hovering over the, as yet, uncreated deep. The source is God, or perhaps it is the point at which the sheer uncreated potential of God meets its own mysterious actualization in creation. It is seedpod at the heartbreaking and glorious moment of generation; it is the welling up of the originating spring, impossible to locate at any point in space, at any moment in time. And in this pilgrimage into the holy land of sources, where knowledge must be intuited rather than secured, it is necessary to recognize (with some regret) that the written word can never be purely 'source' by any stretch of anyone's imagination. This is because it is always an attempted representation of something that precedes it, whether in thought, imagination or in reality. This in itself does not prevent Scripture being attributed the status of 'originating' or 'foundational' document in theology. It does, however, set it realistically into a particular religious and literary context or, more accurately, set of contexts.

It may be more plausible then to view Scripture as an attempt to humanly represent and 'tradition'[7] what is understood of the source and origin, which it does often with great beauty and refinement, than to regard it as source except in the more functional sense of its being 'employed' as such.

Normative Source

This could perhaps mean "a source that establishes a norm or set of norms". It could also mean a document that records the human experience of what it believes to be the originating mystery. If considered 'normative source', this would then be 'employed' definitively to determine practices or behaviours, and/or apprehended dynamically to suggest meaning, mystery and presence. One suspects the term 'normative source' applied too strictly to Holy Scripture, and to its relationship to theology, may smart of reductionism akin to the misrepresentation of sacrament as sign; of divine love as love's all too human expression.

Theology

And now let us turn to what is meant by 'theology'. Theology is faith seeking understanding. It is, traditionally, an academic pursuit that recognizes human deficiency in understanding the divine. It is a laudable pursuit establishing humility, that recognition of one's deficiencies, as a most exquisite thing, and the acquisition of 'understanding' of God as all in all. It is something of the modernist impulse towards deconstruction of these 'givens' that leads to Nietzsche's *Thus Spoke Zarathustra*.[8] Thus, deconstruction can take the theologian into dangerous and sometimes not entirely wholesome waters. But this, too, is necessary in the 'playing out' of what is essentially a risky enterprise of seeking understanding of God. If the theologian does not occasionally venture out beyond the schoolroom or worship space, beyond even the biblical text, s/he will not necessarily know where the ongoing discourse about the created and uncreated, the fathomable and unfathomable is taking place; or, philosophically, where the line between modernism and postmodernism is drawn. This 'inhibited' theologian may not understand that reality is messier than black and white, and more difficult to grasp than the 'one true reading' of the Scriptures.

Footnote

It is important at the outset to recognize anew that all discursive measures—whether of language, art, Scripture, theology or in any other symbol system—may be found to be self-subverting.[9] This does not necessarily lead to nihilism as is sometimes suggested, but to a place where assumptions whether warranted or unwarranted are laid bare. This is a place that begins with the semiological and ends with the ethical. Theology starts at no better place than with an ethical appreciation of the texts that purport to 'found' it, and a realistic appraisal of the "will to power"[10] that can at times underlie the process of interpretation.

"Derived Methodology" (or "What to Make of the Above . . .")

The above exploration of our task—informed as it is by a contemporary consciousness of the status, import, and interpretation of texts—provides a number of ethical constraints that inform the process of considering Scripture as normative source for theology.

First, in treating with the Scriptures it is appropriate to search for meaning and truth, but to assert the uncovering only of meaning. Although within western philosophy the *existence* of pure truth is rarely questioned, the advent of modernist epistemology in the philosophical work of Descartes and Kant led to the questioning of the capacity of human beings to apprehend truth. Modernism has impacted also on biblical studies. During the nineteenth century scriptural texts were contextualized historically, and this led to the concern that tenets appropriate in biblical times would not necessarily be appropriate for the contemporary age. It also led to the recognition that the content of scriptural writings inevitably reflects the views and imperatives of the patriarchal or tribal (and later agricultural) structures of the culture of the author(s). Interest in literary criticism led to valid suspicions about the so-called 'seamless' development of biblical books. It also uncovered the fascinating history of textual compilation. Form criticism led to new strategies of demythologization initiated in the writings of Rudolf Bultmann,[11] whose seminal work questioned the supernatural elements in biblical stories. Add to all of that, the postmodern deconstructive work of linguists, such as Jacques Derrida, that casts doubt on the capacity of language *per se* to convey truth, and it becomes clear that the biblical interpretative enterprise has been led into a condition both of greater freedom and greater complexity. The first is disinclined to uncover 'truth(s)'. The second makes the assertion of truth claims increasingly more difficult. Daniel Migliore recognizes that these challenges within scriptural studies belong to a wider cultural concern to critique authority. He suggests that "Christian faith and theology should honour the good that has accompanied this modern critical spirit, as well as reject the pretensions".[12] He maintains that Scripture should not expect to have "immunity from the wider cultural critique of authority".[13]

The assertion that the Scriptures are somehow *revealed* truth, that they are inspired and therefore free from error, does not really circumvent the difficulties faced by biblical scholars and Christian theologians, as they attempt to interpret their meaning. A faith community might choose to make truth claims about biblical inerrancy, but this is often done through what are considered to be illogical circularities, such as using the Bible itself to determine principles for the interpretation of Scripture.[14] Faith communities are also often not united about exactly what truth claims may be derived from the reading of the Scriptures, and this inconsistency undermines the credibility of any particular 'truth' claimed.

The postmodern theologian does not claim that Scripture contains no truth, but that the vagaries of recollection, writing, reading, and dissemination render it impossible to make *absolute* truth claims out of the text. On a more positive note, the contemporary theologian is likely to consider it appropriate to look to Scripture to learn about the derivation of faith historically, the apprehension of faith personally, and the mystery that seems to undergird these processes.

A second constraint is that it is essential at the outset that the theologian engage the challenge of how it is possible to call the Scriptures *sacred*. It can hardly be argued that the individual words or *pericopae** are sacred, as, clearly, inconsistencies may be found in comparing one biblical account and another. Also, feminist theologian Phyllis Trible has uncovered 'texts of terror' in the Scriptures where violence is wreaked on the innocent (especially women) in ways that would be considered by the contemporary reader to be shocking.[15] It is rather important to understand that the sacredness of the word of God is located within how that Scripture interacts dynamically with Christian individuals and communities within the matrices of meaning and perceived possibility that govern their faith and their lives. These will have evolved for the faithful as functions of tradition, reason and experience, and they are the *loci* of engagement with the Scriptures today. In many ways it seems easier to hang onto the conceit that scriptural authority is invested in the words themselves. It seems riskier to suggest that the sacredness of the Scriptures is located in the dynamic process of reading, marking, learning and inwardly digesting them both in the private and

---

* A selection of text, most often a biblical text, appointed to be read in church or used as a text for a sermon

public sphere.[16] Yet this is clearly the case, as the process of finding inspiration in Scripture is a complex one involving human engagement at every level. Unsurprisingly this is consistent with how the tradition of the Christian Church describes God's ways of addressing humanity, namely through their own humanness. Thus, once again it may be said that biblical interpretation as theological enterprise works according to an incarnational principle. It also works according to the outer and inner workings of the logic of sacramentality, by which a text considered sacred by a faith community functions to bring something of God's presence to that community.[17]

The third ethical constraint is that the theologian, in claiming normativity for Scripture, must recognize that this is not a claim about its content *per se*, as though every word that is scriptural should literally describe a moral or behavioural imperative for today's Christians. Theologians, of course, recognize and respect the canonicity of the Scriptures by which the church has attributed them with foundational authority, albeit that this was determined through all-too-human processes of selection and de-selection. Theologians recognize, too, the definitive place that the Scriptures occupy in the Christian tradition, as the standard for faith and for the development of theological stances or doctrine. The problems with claiming 'normativity'—with its tendency to suggest 'norms' and their 'enforcement'—may be overcome by understanding the 'normative' as evolving through a process of 'traditioning' (as previously indicated); a process that is not static, but ongoing.

Fourthly, theologians must be aware that the Scriptures are a 'source' for theology only in the sense that this is their application. The Bible is not the starting point for a faith, but is expressive of the human experience of God that existed before it was (and while it was being) written. Scripture and tradition are not two separate elements in the process of interpretation to be applied critically to one another. They are integral to one another, as Scripture reflects tradition and shapes it; and as tradition forms Scripture and is formed by it.

A distillation of these concerns leads to the following principles that are helpful in governing the use of Scripture as normative source for theology.

First, it is appropriate to view Scripture as constituting the central text for theology, and to acknowledge that canonicity attributes it with authority in this regard.

Second, theologians must attend to both the cogency and ambiguity of any given text or series of texts; and they should be more invested in uncovering meaning than explicating truth.

Third, there should be an acknowledgement of the power of language, albeit historically contextualized, to suggest meaning to the contemporary reader. Equally there should be recognition of the poverty of language to convey absolute truth for today's Christianity and Church, partly because of its historical contextualization, and partly because of its innate capacity to both represent and usurp representation at the same time.

Fourth, the Scriptures should be considered 'normative source' only in the sense that the Christian tradition has attributed to them this function in the theological enterprise. There should be no 'normativity' that arrogates to itself any claim to power to enforce so called 'norms'. Equally there is no valid concept of text as (innately) 'source', as source and tradition are integral to one another in the processes of the creation and dissemination of Scripture. Thus there should be no necessary literalistic transference of moral codes from the Scriptures unless these are subject to processes of active contemporary critique that are 'well-worked' hermeneutically. Also, assumptions underlying biblical texts that are influenced by attitudes now identified as classist, patriarchal, racist, imperialist and homophobic must be taken into account when evaluating the rightness of deriving moral tenets from biblical material. Migliore acknowledges that "damage can be done when scripture supports coercion, slavery, oppression and terror rather than freedom".[18]

Fifth, there must be room to identify and name mystery, but room also to doubt and critique supernaturalism. John Goldingay's categories of a 'hermeneutics of trust' and a 'hermeneutics of suspicion'[19] are useful in maintaining these two freedoms.

Admittedly these principles may feel unnerving—almost 'edgy'—and they are clearly dependent on interpretative processes that may lead to dissolution as well as resolution. Yet I would maintain that the principles are sound. These principles can be attended to only in the hermeneutical process, as the reader or student or teacher develops the discipline of principled interpretation. This does not diminish the importance of exegesis. Hermeneutics is merely a different (and, often, later) stage of the process of apprehending meaning. Once all that can be is determined about what the original author(s) meant (exegesis), both the authority of their message to speak to the contemporary Church—as well as the limitations attendant on that authority—must be appraised and acknowledged (hermeneutics). Where there is freedom at the hermeneutical end of the process, there is no need for contrivance or artificiality at the exegetical stage. It must not be forgotten that the Christian Scriptures are found to be sacred in the dynamic spiritual processes of writing, revelation and apprehension, by God's grace, for God's holy people, and in keeping with the humility of a God who entrusts to a humanly-derived text and its fallible interpreters the disclosure of the glory of the divine.

How the Scriptures Function
as Normative Source for Christian Theology

The principles derived from the above deconstructive process are ones that, if applied to theological interpretation of the Christian

Scriptures, safeguard both the integrity of the original text, and the freedom of the contemporary interpreter/theologian. They also deter the development of exorbitant claims to truth and inerrancy, and of inappropriate ideas about normativity (as previously defined).

In order to validate these principles, one presupposition must be in place. This is that Scripture is not a self-regulating system characterized by inner consistency, or self-interpretative possibility. Even at times in the history of Christianity when the interpretative freedoms claimed above were not imagined, theologians always looked outside of the text to make sense of the import of the text. And the texts themselves were considered no less enigmatic or elusive, inconsistent or ambiguous, than we find them to be today. If we examine some of the textual material central to the Christological discourses within the early Church, this becomes clear.

It is demonstrable that Church teaching about the person of Christ did not emerge in an uncomplicated way out of the biblical study of the early Church. Scripture suggested that Jesus was a devout follower of the God of Judaism, but not only that. The writers of the New Testament through the telling of stories about his life, and through theological treatises such as those contained in the letters of Paul, seemed to claim for him redemptive significance suggestive of qualities understood to be characteristic of the divine.

The biblical process however was not a neat chronological one within which can be traced a gradual evolution of ideas starting with the identity of Jesus as God's Son, and ending up with doctrinal statements about his divinity. Nor is there a chronological movement from narrative elements describing Jesus' life to proclamatory material making sense of the narratives. It is clear that the gospels contain confessional elements reflecting the faith of the communities out of which they emerged. It is also clear that the earliest texts which could be interpreted as pointing to the divinity of Jesus were probably drawn from liturgical material that would have been in use well before the gospels were written, and centuries before the divinity of Jesus was asserted in doctrinal statements such as those produced by the Council of Nicea in 325 CE.

Examples of liturgical texts of this sort follow. The first is the Psalm text cited in Heb 1:8–9, which recognizes Jesus as the Son of God and suggests a special status for him:

> But of the Son, he (God) says:
> "Your throne O God is [or, God is your throne] for ever and ever,
> and the righteous scepter is the scepter of your kingdom.
> You have loved righteousness and hated wickedness;
> therefore God, your God, has anointed you
> with the oil of gladness beyond your companions."

Jesus' status as son of God the Father is further reinforced in the hymn in John 1:14.

> And the Word became flesh
> and lived among us,
> and we have seen his glory,
> the glory as of a Father's only son,
> full of grace and truth.

In the baptismal formula of Matt 28:19, Jesus is represented as co-equal with God. This is evident long before there is any doctrine associating him with the metaphysics of 'substance' relating to notions of divinity, or suggestive of a trinitarian concept of the godhead: "Go therefore and make disciples of all nations, baptizing them in the name of the Father and of the Son and of the Holy Spirit."

Another text thought to have originated as liturgical material is Col 1:15–20.

> He is the image of the invisible God,
> the first born of all creation;
> for in him all things in heaven and on earth were created,

things visible and invisible,
whether thrones or dominions or rulers or powers—
all things have been created through him and for him.
He himself is before all things,
and in him all things hold together.
He is the head of the body,
the church;
he is the beginning,
the first born from the dead,
so that he might come to have first place in everything.
For in him the fullness of God was pleased to dwell,
and through him God was pleased to reconcile to himself all things,
whether on earth or in heaven,
by making peace through the blood of his cross.

In terms of determining the nature of Christ the first two of these texts are intriguing but ambiguous, attributing 'sonship' to Jesus, but not necessarily divinity. The third is suggestive of a Jesus co-equal with the Father and the Spirit, which may be read to imply divinity, but could be understood in the sense of a son and spirit derived from/by God, but not sharing divinity. The Colossians text displays a heightened rhetoric which describes Jesus as having every possible divine attribute: he is the image of God, Creator of the world, head of the *ekklesia*, occupying first place in everything, in whom God was pleased to dwell, but he is not portrayed explicitly as divine. There is ambiguity in all of these texts, which makes it difficult to 'ground' biblically any Christological claim of divinity.

More ambiguity surrounds the names that were used of Jesus and by Jesus of himself as the New Testament documents bear witness. Jesus was the Messiah, in Greek *Christos*, or "the Christ".[20] This means, literally, "the anointed one". The promised Messiah was the one who would come to release Israel from oppression and rule them in peace as their king. In the gospels,

Peter recognized Jesus as the Messiah (as well as Son): "You are the Messiah, the Son of the living God" (Matt 16:16). Martha also recognized this identity of Jesus: "Yes, Lord, I believe that you are the Messiah, the Son of God, the one who was expected to come into the world" (John 11:27). Yet Jesus never used this terminology when referring to himself. In the Markan account of Jesus' trial however when the high priest asks him, "Are you the Messiah?" Jesus enigmatically says, "I am," and then goes on to employ a different title again—the "Son of Man", which requires its own explication.

Jesus also never referred to himself as God's Son, and always answered ambiguously when others called him this. However a passage from Matthew's gospel does seem to suggest he *thought* of himself as God's Son: "All things have been delivered to me by my Father; and no one knows the Son except the Father, and anyone to whom the Son chooses to reveal him" (Matt 11:27). Also interesting is Jesus' use of the title "Abba" which points to a sense that Jesus had that he was 'son of God' in a special, if undefined, way.

The acknowledgement that "Jesus is Lord" (*kyrios*) is one of the earliest Christian confessions of faith.[21] It had powerful theological associations, because it was used "to translate the Tetragrammaton, the four Hebrew characters (YHWH) used to represent the sacred name of God in the Hebrew Scriptures".[22] The most significant occurrence of the use of the word "Lord" to designate Jesus is found in Phil 2:9–11, a passage which is very early—probably pre-Pauline—yet which has a developed sense of possibility that Jesus might have divine attributes.[23]

> Therefore God also highly exalted him
> and gave him the name that is above every name,
> so that at the name of Jesus every knee should bend,
> in heaven and on earth and under the earth,
> and every tongue should confess
> that Jesus Christ is Lord
> to the glory of God the Father.

Here the early Christian writer takes a Hebrew Bible declaration (Isa 45:23) that every knee will bow to the Lord God, and transfers it to the Lord Jesus Christ, which again *suggests* the divinity of Jesus without *claiming* it explicitly.[24]

The term "Son of Man" is possibly the most difficult of the titles of Jesus to interpret, because the scholarship that examines it is not conclusive. Apart from a few exceptions, Jesus is the one who uses this title in the New Testament: seventy times in the Synoptic Gospels and twelve in the Gospel of John. In two places the titles are used by others (Acts 7:56; John 12:34). Jesus never claims to be "Son of Man", but there are times when the gospels seem to portray him as referring to himself when he uses it (Matt 8:20; Mark 8:31). On the other hand the term "Son of Man" in common usage in Jesus' day often implied simply the sense of "I". It is possible that Jesus used this title in this rather mundane way, and the early church invested it with apocalyptic meaning.

Theologians of the early Church—searching within the above range of vital liturgical New Testament texts suggestive of Jesus' divinity—might themselves be convicted of that claim, but their theological task was not assisted by the essential inconsistency and ambiguity of the texts themselves. And the history of the first few centuries of the Christian Church tells us that despite the plethora of such reverential texts, the issue of whether or not Jesus was divine was hugely controversial. Arian and his followers disputed the divinity of Jesus; Athanasius averred it. These men were contemporaries, respected leaders of the Church, and theologians of the same city of Alexandria. They were familiar with the same philosophical thought-forms and they used the same Scriptures to form the basis of their theological views. Demonstrably, then, the truth of Jesus' divinity was not derived from scriptural material in an uncomplicated manner, as though it lay, a clear theological concept, a glittering jewel, merely to be mined, extracted, from the text. It was deliberated upon, thought about and prayed (and fought) over for centuries. The ignominious 'will to power' later articulated by the philosopher Nietzsche displayed the full force of its ire in a history of exclusion and belittlement meted out by both sides.[25]

If the Scriptures serve as a normative source for theology, it is clear that they have not been applied exclusively in doctrinal development. Clearly a series of early liturgical affirmations at once uplifting and ambiguous, and a set of different titles for Jesus that were inconsistent, and again ambiguous, could hardly by themselves lead to the formation of the well-worked metaphysical formulae that took on the status of Christological doctrine in the fourth century. This is, namely, that Jesus was "one in essence/substance" (consubstantial/*homoousios*) with the Father,[26] and not "of similar substance" (*homoiousios*). And that Jesus was one person with two natures, human and divine so that a distinction within Christ was placed squarely on the level of nature while the unity resided fully in the sphere of the person.[27] Clearly this Christology emerged out of more than a dispassionate appraisal of the relevant scriptural texts. The process involved interpretation of the text that would have engaged what I have referred to above as "matrices of meaning and perceived possibility" as these existed for individual theologians and their immediate faith communities. It is also indisputable that the formation of these definitive doctrines about the person of Christ were as much dependent on the philosophical milieu of the day within which an Aristotelian system of metaphysics (characterized by concepts of essence/substance) was dominant.[28]

Conclusion

This chapter has developed a set of interpretative principles derived from deconstructive impulses found within certain areas of semiotics. It maintains that the application of these will preserve integrity of scriptural texts as well as offer freedom to theologians interpreting Scripture in order to form theological propositions and insights. It is comfortable with the tendency to understand Scripture as 'normative source' in theology on the condition that 'normativity' is redefined in terms of 'suggestion of meaning' rather than 'enforcement of truth'. The discussion also demonstrates that in the development of early Christology Scripture has not provided an unambiguous or self-referential system. The theological enterprise has thus often taken into account categories both cultural and philosophical that explicate the interpreted sense of the biblical text without much direct reference to its specific language or concepts. An application of the principles suggested may seem 'edgy' for theology, but their outworking remains part of a tradition of interpretation which conditions 'normativity' in terms of contemporary philosophical and interpretative mores.

Notes

1. See Saussure, *Writings in General Linguistics*, Spivak, Introduction, in Derrida, *Of Grammatology*, xliii.

2. On the terminology used by Ludwig Wittgenstein and Mikhail Baktin, see Conner, *Postmodern Culture*, 203.

3. Moments of particular theological insight that engage the whole personality, including the feelings. See Lonergan, *Love and Objectivity in Virtue Ethics*, 37.

4. A form of words used to describe the nature of sacramental presence in Lutheran writings.

5. English folk song suggesting playfulness and mischievousness, hopefully to be found present in the Church of God. Also a mark of the inclusion of 'pastiche' characteristics of postmodern discourses and other 'productions'. For lyrics and music see: http://www.folkinfo.org/songs/displaysong.php?songid=195.

6. Williams, *On Christian Theology*, 45.

7. A term introduced by Brueggeman, *Introduction to the Old Testament*, to describe the process of interpreting Scripture to make it alive today.

8. Nietzsche, *Thus Spoke Zarathustra*, Prologue §3. In this work Nietzsche introduces the concept of *Übermensch*, or "superman", implying the idealization of human self-mastery/self-cultivation/self-direction. This work also contains the famous dictum, "God is dead."

9. This is part of the critique of metaphysics that arguably began in the work of Immanuel Kant, and found expression in the postmodern

era through the semiotic work of Ferdinand De Saussure, Jacques Derrida and Roland Barthes.

10. Nietzsche, *Thus Spoke Zarathustra,* Part I §15. Innate and all-consuming human desire for power.

11. See Bultmann, *History of the Synoptic Tradition.*

12. Migliore, *Faith Seeking Understanding,* 45.

13. Migliore, *Faith Seeking Understanding,* 45.

14. See John Goldingay's critique of B. B. Warfield, "Inspiration and Inerrancy" in *Models for Scripture,* 267.

15. Trible, *Texts of Terror.*

16. *Book of Common Prayer* (1662), Collect for the Second Sunday in Advent.

17. Schneiders, *The Revelatory Text,* 40–43.

18. Migliore, *Faith Seeking Understanding,* 46–47.

19. Goldingay, *Models for Interpretation of Scripture,* 48.

20. McGrath, *Christian Theology,* 351.

21. McGrath, *Christian Theology,* 354.

22. McGrath, *Christian Theology,* 354.

23. McGrath, *Christian Theology,* 354.

24. McGrath, *Christian Theology,* 354.

25. The Council of Constantinople (381 CE) made a point of systematically denouncing Eunomians or Anomeans; Arians or Eudoxians; Semi-Arians or Pneumatomachs; Sabellians, Marcellians, Photinians; and Apollinarists—all those who did not agree with the prevailing voice of the gathering. Athanasius was deposed and restored to his see several times as he held to his Christological viewpoint; and Arius was deemed a heretic at the first Council of Nicea, later exonerated at the first Synod of Tyre (335 CE), and after his death was pronounced a heretic again at the Council of Constantinople.

26. Council of Nicea (325 CE).

27. Council of Chalcedon (451 CE).

28. McIntyre, *Shape of Christology,* 87.

3

Wisdom as well as Facts

Steven Ogden

The Story Rings True

Unique to the Gospel of Luke, the Parable of the Lost Son can be read as a compelling existential drama (Luke 15:11–32). From the start, a sense of apprehension is evoked as the younger of two sons demands his "share of the property" (v. 12). Half-expected, a tragedy unfolds that is both heart-rending and humanizing as the son squanders everything and ends up feeding the pigs (v. 16). Ironically, the crisis creates a small space for self-awareness to emerge, gently prying open the reader as well as the son (v. 17: "he came to himself"). The son stoically, perhaps bravely, returns to the father. Expecting to be put in a lowly place, the son is given pride of place at a feast, which is held in his honour (v. 23: "a robe—the best one"). Generously, the father spells out the transformative significance of what has just transpired "for this son of mine was dead and is alive again; he was lost and is found" (v. 24; cf. Luke 19:10).

The story has reached its climax, engendering hope in listeners and readers alike, maybe proffering new insights into the heart of God. But is this the climax? What about the sting in the tale? After all, the elder son is aggrieved (v. 28). Ironically, the elder son had everything, but nothing (v. 31). Blind to the possibilities of life, he was unable to rejoice with his younger brother (v. 32). For these reasons, the parable could be read as the story of the elder son. Besides, as is often the case, the subtext is often the real text. In short, this is a great story, pregnant with interpretive twists, theological insights and potential flights of fancy. But

43

what kind of a text is it? And is it true? Perhaps naively, I have taken the parable at face value as a parable. It is not a historical account about an ancient family. However, if the story is not historical, does this mean it is not true? At one level, if what is true is defined in strictly empirical terms, the parable is palpably not true. It is just a parable. At another level, I cannot dismiss this parable as untrue, simply because there is a lack of corroborating empirical data. More to the point, the significant things in my life concern human relationships and personal meaning. Their significance is not exclusively bound to empirical controls, strong arguments or hard evidence.

John 1:1–18 (the prologue), compared with the Parable of the Lost Son, is of a different order. Truth, in the context of the parable, has to do with the reader making personal connections with the story's characters and gleaning general theological insights on the basis of the father's behaviour. John's prologue, however, is making a claim about the person of Jesus. The prologue is probably an early hymn, celebrating the Incarnation, using ancient tropes to interpret the existential and symbolic import of Jesus. Arguably the hymn, especially as it has been embedded in John's narrative, makes (proto-ontological) claims about the identity of Jesus ("the Word became flesh").[1] Nevertheless, "the Word" in the text does not relate directly to the Jesus of history. Moreover, the doctrine of the Incarnation itself, even in its earliest forms, cannot be subjected fruitfully to the scrutiny of historiography. Therefore, on epistemological grounds, the prologue can be dismissed as liturgical refinement or theological invention. But is it so simple? The question of truth in biblical interpretation is complex and a narrow historicist approach is not up to the task.

Currently, there is a battle in the public square over the authority of Scripture. My concern with this controversy is that time and energy are misspent in an unwinnable war. As a result, and in the name of truth, truth has become a casualty. I say "public square" because the debate is more nuanced in the ivory towers of biblical scholarship, than in public jousting, media events and meretricious sound bites. However, to illustrate the character of this polemic, let me make a stark contrast between the antagonists.

In one corner is Christian fundamentalism.[2] In general, fundamentalists can be characterized by a particular view of truth, where truth is universal, absolute, identifiable, and in their possession. In this context, and in circular fashion, the Bible is used selectively to support truth claims, which are used in turn to bolster the epistemological authority of the Bible or the ecclesial authority of the Bible teacher. In the other corner, there are exponents of what could be broadly described as progressive biblical scholarship. In general, the progressives can be characterized by a particular view of truth, where the epistemological value of a biblical text is carefully measured on the basis of historical method and corresponding empirical evidence. If a story cannot be empirically substantiated, it is not true. Truth here is context-specific, relative, identifiable and in their possession. In particular, if truth is understood exclusively in historical terms, then the Parable of the Lost Son is either not true or of less (epistemological) value than historical facts. In both cases, fundamentalist and progressive, there is an element of epistemological naiveté. Interpretation of a text is not neat or straightforward (cf. J. Derrida) and the generation of truth statements is even more complex (cf. R. Rorty).

In this chapter, I am interested in the progressive position. I think it has a lot to offer, but its approach is hamstrung by a limited view of history, epistemology, experience, and hermeneutics. So I want to make a few modest suggestions as to how the progressive position may prosper. In order to do this, I will explore briefly the notions of history, truth and experience. Throughout, it is important to keep a weather eye on the discipline of history: what is it, and what is its epistemological role in biblical studies?

In other words, how does history establish truth statements in biblical studies? In preparation, and as a means of crystallizing issues further, I want to look at an older version of the debate.

An Old Problem Revisited

In the middle of the last century, two formidable theologians were wrestling independently with similar issues, namely Paul Tillich (1886–1965) and Karl Rahner (1904–1984).[3] I have a personal interest in these 'German Shepherds' of the faith, but at times, they both ran the risk of selling theology short by over-emphasizing the importance of history as the medium, in which theology is expressed, at the expense of theology getting its facts right. They favoured a macro-view of history, over a micro-view.

Tillich and Rahner were interested in history. In particular, they were interested in working out their theologies in, and for, the real (historical) world. However, they saw themselves working primarily as theologians and presumed theology had a different set of objectives to history. Moreover, they were reacting to and against the historical positivism of their day. The formative period for Tillich and Rahner was between "the first and the second quest, which began with the work of Martin Kähler in 1896 and ended with Ernst Käsemann's revival of historical-Jesus research in 1953".[4] In that time, they were part of a theological movement that was sceptical about the promised outcomes of the quest for the historical Jesus. Specifically, they were critics of historical reductionism and—at this level—this makes them precursors of postmodernity.

Tillich argued that research into the historical Jesus had failed.[5] For him, the reality of the 'Christ-event' was actualized by faith through human participation; it was not captive to the particulars of historical research.[6] Besides, is it really possible to get behind a biblical text, via historical criticism, to the historical Jesus, because the Jesus in the texts is the Christ of faith? Tillich claims,

Faith can say that the reality which is manifest in the New Testament picture of Jesus as the Christ has saving power for those who are grasped by it, no matter how much or how little can be traced to the historical figure who is called Jesus of Nazareth.[7]

Likewise, Rahner accepted the general findings of modern scientific exegesis about the life of Jesus.[8] However, he asserted that the limits of exegesis were determined by dogmatics; this meant he interpreted exegetical findings from within the dogmatic setting of salvation history.[9] For Rahner, dogmatics includes the a priori (transcendental) level of analysis, whereas exegesis concentrates on the a posteriori (categorical) level.[10]

In brief, Tillich and Rahner had a commitment to the importance of history and considered the results of New Testament exegesis important. They had a macro-view of history as God's medium of self-disclosure. But this raises a problem, in that, while they thought it was important for Christology to be grounded in exegetical findings, they did not feel bound to them. Neither of them resolved this grey area. In fairness, the relationship between historical figure and salvific figure, where a text is the primary source, is complex. Moreover, history is not the same as a narrative that captures something of experience and has an epistemological contribution to make.[11] However, if some progressives overestimate the potential contribution of historical research, Tillich and Rahner ran the risk of underestimating its value.

History Has Its Problems

In some theologically conservative circles, the assumption has been made that recourse to history will remedy deficiencies in theological knowledge; that is, if there is a credibility gap (e.g. the resurrection) then a piece of historical evidence might address it (e.g. the empty tomb). In other cases, an over-reliance on history can be seen to undermine the credibility of orthodox beliefs; that is, if history can explain everything, then there is no room for faith (e.g. miracle stories dismissed). Progressives have also relied too much on history. History has its own problems. In particular, the field of history has been subject to hermeneutical problems similar to those that have assailed theology.

In history, there is wide recognition of the problems associated with the nature of facts, the interpretation of facts and the development of narratives. Be that as it may, I am not going to the other extreme of arguing that facts cannot be established and it is all a matter of alternative readings: "Even consciously postmodernist reconstructionists are trying to help us to form *better* beliefs about what they think actually happened."[12] So it is important at this juncture to clarify the limits of history. In his classic study, E. H. Carr cast a critical eye over historiography.[13] Carr questioned the efforts of certain nineteenth-century historians who searched for historical facts. He questioned assumptions such as facts being 'readily identifiable', the facts 'speaking for themselves', or that history is 'an accumulation of facts'.

Carr was critical of static or empirical approaches to history. In contrast, he offers a dynamic view of interpretation.[14] His view is based on a number of interactive relationships between fact and interpretation as well as past, present, and future. In this context, he claims that the historian is part of history.[15] Thus, it is important to understand the historian as well as the historian's social and historical context. Further, the historian needs to establish reliable standards and tests of significance, because interpretation entails selection on the historian's part and selection is based on significance "as determined and attributed by the historian".[16] Consequently,

> History requires the selection and ordering of facts about the past in the light of some principle or norm of objectivity accepted by the historian, which necessarily includes elements of interpretation. Without this, the past dissolves into a jumble of innumer-

able isolated and insignificant incidents, and history cannot be written at all.[17]

Since the publication of Carr's book, recognition of the role of the interpreter has grown, regardless of whether the interpreter is a historian, a theologian or a philosopher. This raises problems. For Scott,

> History is in the paradoxical position of creating the objects it claims only to discover. By creating, I don't mean making things up, but rather constructing them as legitimate and coherent objects of knowledge.[18]

Some scholars have taken this even further. For Oakeshott, the past is understood as a construction based on the present.[19] The past is not simply appropriated by the present; it is shaped by the present. According to Oakeshott, historiography is a type of thinking, or an attitude towards history, which produces its own peculiar form of discourse. Unlike scientific discourse, historical discourse cannot establish necessary and sufficient conditions for truth statements. Critically, history deals with occasions, and so it has to wrestle with contingent truths.

Burke claims there is a new kind of history-writing emerging in which culture is one of the driving forces,

> The philosophical foundation of the new history is the idea that reality is socially or culturally constituted. . . . This relativism also undermines the traditional distinction between what is central in history and what is peripheral.[20]

The so-called 'new history' is plausible. In this light, it is reasonable to speak of the crisis of the traditional paradigm of historical writing, but "the new paradigm also has its problems: problems of definition, problems of sources, problems of method, problems of explanation".[21] Clearly, there are problems in the field of history that need to be addressed. These problems often require a reading between the lines by the interpreter. But on what basis should this reading be conducted? Burke concludes, "The discipline of history is now more fragmented than ever before."[22] In short, here is pause for thought. History, as a discipline, is going through changes. This does not mean biblical scholars and theologians should abandon it, but rather, it is important to use it wisely, within the context of a broader understanding of method.

What Is Truth?

The concept of truth is complicated. For Nietzsche, truth is far from certain. For Rorty, truth cannot be clinically separated from the inquirer; by virtue of the fact that truth is always presented in the form of a description. Even a physicist, who is part of a particular scientific community, interprets results and writes reports. And it is even more complicated in non-science communities.

> Truth cannot be out there—cannot exist independently of the human mind—because sentences cannot so exist, or be out there. The world is out there, but descriptions of the world are not. Only descriptions of the world can be true or false. The world on its own—unaided by the describing activities of human beings—cannot.[23]

The search for an adequate definition of truth is part of the modern quest for certainty. Thus, scientists use probability statements, which apply under certain conditions, until the arrival of new and/or contrary results. But any mode of inquiry has its limitations. After all, there is the way that the world is:

> This does not mean that our procedures for warranting assertions cannot attain truth. But it does mean that we cannot be *absolutely certain* they do because reality always outstrips our modes of inquiry.[24]

So, in this chapter, when it comes to truth, there is no epistemic cure-all. There is, however, a pragmatic preference for a form of coherence (e.g. facts-interpretation-communal experience).[25]

> There is no "purely conceptual" discipline, which deals only in timeless, a priori knowledge. However, if we are right that beliefs

are justified by their coherence with other beliefs and that justification is essentially public and social, then there is still a great deal to be understood and explained.[26]

Experience is hard to define. It can be expressed in and shaped by language. It is belief-like in character. It can also be expressed in propositions. But it is more than a series of propositions, as justification "depends on experiential evidence and reasons working together".[27] Certainly, experience by itself does not justify belief.[28] Nonetheless, there is need for practical wisdom. For example, in daily life, I know a particular object is a hammer, and hammers are for hammering nails, because, unless I am dreaming, I have picked it up and used it. It works. At that level, it is true. It is true because it works. For most of us, this is the test we use every day. And it is a remarkably reliable test.

In general, the meaning of *experience* includes "putting to the test, proof by trial, an interior state of being and personal knowledge".[29] It connotes a subject, subjects and a world. There is also a technical nuance, where experience has to do with observation, knowledge and sense experience. Philosophically, experience is associated with empiricism. In its naïve form, empiricism reduces experience to sense data and presumes there is a simple correlation between object and sense data (cf. certain progressives). But how is the correlation made? Who makes it? Clearly, sense data are important, but there is more to experience than what is conveyed by the term 'sense data'.[30]

In this chapter, *experience* is used in two senses. The first sense of experience is the objective sense, for example, sociological information about the *Jewishness* of Jesus.[31] The second sense of experience is the subjective sense. Often the subjective sense is dismissed out of hand, but it has an important place in a theological epistemology. As Alston argues:

> I want to make a start at defending the idea that the experience of God, or, as I shall say, the *perception* of God plays an epistemic role with respect to beliefs about God importantly analogous to

that played by sense perception with respect to beliefs about the physical world.[32]

Alston is not ignoring the differences between sense perception and the perception of God. Instead, he is arguing that, on the basis of similarities between sense perception and the perception of God, there is a case for considering that the idea of the experience of God is worthy of epistemic consideration. This is the key, and it is in this sense that we say a story rings true or that a story has epistemological significance. In other words, historical evidence is scarce for major Christological themes (cf. the Incarnation). However, there is the experience of the early church as found in Scripture and tradition. This does not mean, however, that just because a disciple, a gospel writer or an early theologian thinks something is true, that it is true. In terms of justifying theological beliefs, the subjective sense of experience alone is inadequate without additional qualification and support: "Experience, however, does not settle the matter because the justification of any proposition involves the support of other beliefs as well."[33] Further, by experience, I am not talking about the lone (male) heroes of the faith. So, experience may include the ancient authority figures, from Paul to Augustine and beyond, but real epistemological *clout* comes from contemporary, corporate, intersubjective experience.

A Working Epistemology

The aim of this section is to develop a working model of epistemology. To begin, this needs to be put in context. This chapter presumes that the findings of biblical studies and theology are provisional and existence is 'contingent'. Contingency is used in two ways. First, it is used in a broad theological/metaphorical sense to suggest that the quest for certainty is fraught with difficulties and there is always an element of doubt. Secondly, it is used in a philosophical sense to say that truth claims are not made here in absolute terms; they are expressed in terms of probability. Most of all, the chapter's understanding of experience recognizes that there is a place in epistemology for social and public factors.[34]

Experience has a role in contributing to knowledge, but the meaning of the concept of knowledge is problematic, especially given that philosophers cannot agree about the meaning and value of epistemology. All this makes for a note of caution about pronouncing anything more than a working definition of knowledge. Nonetheless, this does not mean epistemological considerations are treated lightly. In this chapter, the acquisition of new knowledge is understood in incremental terms, as part of an ongoing conversation, expressed in terms of probability-like statements. The term 'incremental' is used in a post-metaphysical sense of not seeking to create new absolutes nor revert to old ones. In particular, the term refers to the cumulative nature of the process of acquiring new knowledge, which is step-by-step, piece-by-piece, over time and in conversation with other voices. It is a "method of successive approximation".[35] This represents a shift in expectations from the ambitious *modern* expectation of establishing a comprehensive fail-safe epistemological *system* (cf. grand narratives) to a cumulative *process* that canvasses incremental and collaborative increases in knowledge (cf. wisdom). So how do increments in new knowledge cohere and in what way does that represent true knowledge?

Concerning the accumulation of knowledge—the step-by-step, piece-by-piece process—C. S. Peirce posits the metaphor of a cable, where the strength of the cable is based on the number of fibres and their interconnections.[36] Similarly, J. Armstrong describes the accumulation of knowledge this way,

> This might be called Venetian Justification. There is no solid ground upon which the city is built. But by way of millions of piers driven into the lagoon it does actually (still) stand, although no pier on its own can be thought of as uniquely supporting it.[37]

Likewise, Susan Haack,

My approach will be informed by the analogy of a crossword puzzle—where there is undeniably pervasive mutual support among entries but, equally undeniably, no vicious circle. The clues are the analog of experiential evidence, already-completed intersecting entries the analog of reasons. As how reasonable a crossword entry is depends both on the clues and on other intersecting entries, the idea is, so how justified an empirical belief is depends on experiential evidence and reasons working together.[38]

With the three images (i.e., cable, Venice, crossword puzzle), knowledge is cumulative and dependent on a degree of coherence between various beliefs (i.e., fibres, piers, clues). The term 'conversation' presumes the accumulation of knowledge will take place by means of a process of dialogue with other 'voices' (e.g., historical, theological, cultural, and ecclesial). In other words, "justification is essentially public and social".[39] Likewise, but from a different perspective, Rorty claims "justification is not a matter of a special relation between ideas (or words) and objects, but of conversation, of social practice".[40] The epistemology in this chapter includes a place for conversation as well as other factors. Conversation, however, does not ensure justified true belief, but it militates against a simplistic correlation between a belief and a "simple bit of direct experiential evidence".[41] In our context, wisdom is more than just a simple bit of direct experiential evidence.

Possibilities

The current polemic between fundamentalists and progressives over biblical interpretation runs the risk of treating truth and experience inadequately, with both parties operating out of a form of reductionism. To reiterate, this is a modern problem. Admittedly, there is disagreement about the meaning of postmodernity, but there is agreement that the term 'modernity' no longer suits our era. In addition, the pursuit of the modern problem gives tacit approval to the Enlightenment's bifurcation of matter and spirit (subject and object). Unthinking attachment to modernity's way of seeing the world stems in part from the success of empirical approaches, which emerged from the Enlightenment (cf. sciences). These approaches have a particular way of seeing the world, with method and procedures to match, which involve testing and re-testing. And it works. Moreover, the so-called empirical approach has already made a contribution to a range of disciplines, including biblical studies and theology. For instance, the impact of archaeological discoveries, sociological reconstructions, and historical evidence has been enormous. But biblical studies and theology are not sciences *per se*. What is more, the full value of contemporary biblical studies will not be realized by the rigid application of a narrow form of empiricism to a broad and complex set of sacred texts.

This chapter's comparison between fundamentalists and progressives is a typology. The contrast raises important issues, but the world, even the theological world, is more complex than this. So it is important to make four qualifications. First, the intensity fuelling the debate is related to the fact that the so-called *third quest* for the historical Jesus has captured the public imagination, and there is nothing like success to bring out detractors.[42] Second, and positively, the quest reflects a renewed sense of confidence in history and historical methods. Third, and negatively, the polemic reflects modernity's quest for, and angst about, certainty. Finally, in practice the debate is finely nuanced. There is disagreement among scholars themselves. For example, Mack asserts that the importance of Jesus "as a thinker and teacher can certainly be granted and even greatly enhanced once we allow the thought that Jesus was not a god incarnate but a real historical person".[43] In contrast, Johnson's criticism of the third quest concerns historical reductionism.[44] For him, progressives are in danger of granting history foundational status.[45] Johnson is half-right, but he is at risk of underestimating the value of the specific contributions history makes to biblical studies (cf. Tillich and Rahner).

The progressive movement has much to offer, but its approach is constrained by a limited view of history, epistemology, experience, and hermeneutics. In particular, it simplifies history and overestimates its contribution. In contrast, I am making a modest claim for experience and its epistemological significance in interpreting texts. A story like the Parable of the Lost Son has epistemological significance partly because it rings true with shared human experience. In Foucauldian terms, it comes out of, and makes sense within, the discursive practices of living Christian communities, where texts are more than historical artefacts.

So, there is an important place for truth statements in the study of the Scriptures, and many scholars are aware of this. But what does it mean to talk about epistemology in the interpretation of Scriptures? Epistemology is related to the idea of establishing new knowledge, which is true knowledge. If epistemology is narrowly defined in empirical terms, however, then a text like John's prologue has little or no value. But most of us expect more from a reading of Scripture than the results of a limited version of empiricism. So what more can be said about a text, like the prologue, which constitutes true knowledge? This is where experience comes in. In particular, the fact that the process of garnering new knowledge is a *mediated* process is critical.

Living, loving, thinking human beings—including biblical scholars—interpret facts out of their experience, and from within personal, social, and professional contexts. Thus, the interpretation of facts is mediated by experience (subjective as well as objective). The reality of mediation, however, does not minimize the significance of facts. Instead, it highlights the importance of critically understanding the place of facts in the process of interpretation. Fact finding, even in physics, involves personal and corporate experience (cf. T. Kuhn). In biblical studies, moreover, experience is conducive for the discernment of new wisdom.

The significance of facts is not trivialized, because their interpretation implies a process of mediation. On the contrary, the full significance of facts is mined from the process of interpretation. In a theological context, this is the role of wisdom. Wisdom involves critical reflection about facts and their meaning. Thus, sapiential insights—through sayings, stories and symbols—transcend the import of individual and separate pieces of evidence. In order to do this today, we have to create space in hermeneutics for the contribution of experience. This is not a neat process, but in many ways, it is more realistic. In so doing, it reminds us that facts find their meaning in communities. Indeed facts have no intrinsic meaning outside of living, interpreting communities. To appreciate this, let us return to the parable and to the prologue, and begin to explore interpretive possibilities. Of course, within the confines of this chapter, this is at best a hint, a creative suggestion. However, there is much at stake in the controversy over Scripture, and that makes these possibilities worth exploring.

Is the Parable of the Lost Son 'just' a parable? The answer is 'yes' and 'no'. Yes, it is a parable, which does not reflect the life and times of an actual family. No, it is not just a parable, simply because there is a lack of evidence. Further, the significant things in life concern relationships and meaning. In the end, the Parable of the Lost Son rings true with experience. Truth, in this setting, has to do with the reader making personal connections with the story's characters and gleaning theological insights, particularly on the basis of the father's behaviour. But it is more than this. In the world of the parable, the younger son's *new perception* (v. 17: "when he came to himself") creates the possibility of a *new experience* (v. 20: his father "ran and put his arms around him and kissed him").[46]

Consider the bottom line and assume the parable does not come from the lips of Jesus, but emerges from an early church community. So, the parable expresses the shared memory of a faith community. Its placement in the gospel presents the figure of Jesus as a messenger and a model for a new way of living. Through the experience of the reign of God, which for them was proclaimed and embodied by the historical Jesus, there is potential for transformation. In other words, it is about *new perceptions* leading to *new experiences.* In and by itself, the parable does not constitute a complete or unambiguous truth statement. But this faith community bears witness to the historical Jesus as a source of transformation, because its shared memory has been enshrined in and enlivened by the narrative context. The story is an existential expression of that witness. The content of the experience is up for debate, but the fact that their experience finds concrete expression, in a parable, is a historical reality. Presuming we are no longer captive to modernity's bifurcation of the material and the spiritual, there is wisdom here. Moreover, the elder son's response not only emphasizes the complexity and ambiguity of human relationships, but it serves to underline the importance of the transformative experience.

John 1:1–18 is a complex example, but like the parable, truth has to do with the wisdom of a particular faith community. This involves the concrete, critical, and corporate reflection on experience, which finds new life in narrative form. Unlike the parable, however, John's prologue is making a claim about *the person* of Jesus. Ironically, the fact that the prologue is arguably based on an early hymn, using ancient tropes to interpret the significance of Jesus, serves to underline the wisdom-making process. So where does history come in? Certainly, the historical Jesus did not write the prologue and the prologue is not a *historical* description of Jesus of Nazareth. But it does reflect the wisdom-making processes of a historic faith community, which is grounded in the memory of a historic figure, and given new life in a living narrative tradition.

Within the confines of this chapter, I can only make a general critique and offer a few hints for future reflection. To express something more tangible, however, and in keeping with the theme of experience, I want to refer to a liturgical example. In many Churches, John's prologue is read on Christmas Eve during the service of lessons and carols, or on Christmas Day. It is a remarkable corporate experience. It does not *prove* the doctrine of the Incarnation, but it rings true with the faith community.

In that inspired reading-in-community, the faithful feel, apprehend, even claim that the historical Jesus has contemporary existential significance. In and of itself, the *text* is not a historical fact. However, that this reading-in-community has power for real people is a fact that deserves to be part of the epistemological equation. This is not the same as saying, because a faith community believes something, it is true. It is saying, however, that just as experience has a role in a contemporary liturgy or an early Church hymn, it also has a role in contemporary biblical interpretation. Today, there are many within and without the Church, who want to know the facts. This is important. But we must take the next step and open the doors for wisdom.

Notes

1. This can be regarded as a proto-ontological claim, reflecting on the identity of Jesus, since it anticipates the emergence of the Church's doctrine of the Incarnation.

2. In Australia, a 'conservative evangelical' is not necessarily fundamentalist. The difference hinges largely on epistemology.

3. For a detailed account of epistemology and experience, see Ogden, *The Presence of God in the World*.

4. Schüssler Fiorenza, "Jesus of Nazareth in Historical Research", 33.

5. Tillich, *Systematic Theology*, vol. 1, 105.

6. Tillich, *Systematic Theology*, vol. 1, 114.

7. Tillich, *The Dynamics of Faith*, 88.

8. Rahner, *Foundations of Christian Faith*, 247.

9. Rahner, "Remarks on the Importance of the History of Jesus", 208.

10. Rahner, "The Position of Christology in the Church", 194.

11. Fredriksen, "What Does Jesus Have to Do with Christ?", 6; and McEvoy, "Narrative or History?", 279–80.

12. Butler, *Postmodernism*, 35.

13. Carr, *What is History?*

14. Carr, *What is History?*, 24.

15. Carr, *What is History?*, 38.

16. Carr, *What is History?*, 118–19.

17. Carr, *What is History?*, lxi, from Carr's notes for the proposed second edition.

18. Scott, "After History?", 1.

19. Oakeshott, "The Activity of Being an Historian", 69–95.

20. Burke, "Overture", 3–4.

21. Burke, "Overture", 9.

22. Burke, "Overture", 18.

23. Rorty, *Contingency, Irony and Solidarity*, 5.

24. Kane, "The Ends of Metaphysics", 420.

25. Everitt and Fisher, *Modern Epistemology*, 202–3.

26. Everitt and Fisher, *Modern Epistemology*, 208.

27. Haack, "A Foundherentist Theory of Empirical Justification", 242.

28. Haack, *Evidence and Inquiry*, 187. The cause of an experience is not necessarily a form of justification.

29. *The New Shorter Oxford English Dictionary.*

30. Everitt and Fisher, *Modern Epistemology*, 72.

31. Crossan, *The Historical Jesus*, 421.

32. Alston, "The Autonomy of Religious Experience", 67, 86.

33. Keating, "Epistemology and the Theological Application of Jesus Research", 34–35.

34. Everitt and Fisher, *Modern Epistemology*, 202–3, 207–8.

35. Haack, *Evidence and Inquiry*, 73.

36. Peirce, "Some Consequences of Four Incapacities", 157 [265].

37. Armstrong, *Looking at Pictures*, 151.

38. Haack, "A Foundherentist Theory", 242.

39. Everitt and Fisher, *Modern Epistemology*, 208.

40. Rorty, *Philosophy and the Mirror of Nature*, 170.

41. Rorty, *Philosophy and the Mirror of Nature*, 226n6.

42. Johnson, *The Real Jesus*, 32. Johnson dismissively refers to Spong as an amateur representative of the third quest. Fiorenza has a more constructive description of the quest in "Jesus of Nazareth", 34–37.

43. Mack, *Who Wrote the New Testament?*, 47.

44. Johnson, *The Real Jesus*, 2 and 5. According to Johnson, the New Testament offers the *real* Jesus. This is what the Church experiences. However, he does not adequately define the real Jesus.

45. Johnson, *The Real Jesus*, 112. Johnson argues they do not adequately treat the narrative framework of the Gospels, as a framework can be established using lines of convergence, cf. Schüssler Fiorenza "Jesus of Nazareth", 33.

46. In *Love Upside Down* I explore the relationship between new perception and experience in the context of contemporary ethical issues.

4

Scripture, God-Talk and Jesus

Nigel Leaves

Human Words about Who We Think God Is

Early in the first meeting of an Introduction to Theology course, a university lecturer is likely to announce that the Bible is not the literal Word of God and then go on to explain that it is a collection of literary documents reflecting diverse historical/social contexts and containing the writings of human authors engaged in a search for God. This way of understanding/interpreting texts comes as such a shock to some that it shakes the foundations of their faith, but most welcome the confirmation that the Bible includes a plurality of theologies. After years of unsuccessful attempts to reconcile incompatible concepts of God, these students understand the Scriptures to be human reflections on the nature of the Divine; and are thereby enabled to undertake critical analyses of the numerous theologies represented within the sixty-six books that constitute the Bible.[1] At last they can admit what has long been clear to many of us:

> There has never been a 'right' way of viewing God. . . . The Bible does not attest a single view of God. Rather one finds in its pages multiple views—for example, the capricious God of Job, the unconscionable God of 1 Samuel 15 who ordered the annihilation of the Amalekites, and the ethical God of the Hebrew prophets.[2]

More importantly, this approach introduces students to the process of carefully scrutinizing each author's understanding of

63

God and thus avoiding a common literary fallacy—one recently committed by the highly regarded evolutionary biologist Richard Dawkins. In his oft-quoted rant against the God of the Hebrew Bible—whom he describes as "arguably the most unpleasant character in all fiction: jealous and proud of it; a petty, unjust, unforgiving control-freak; a vindictive, bloodthirsty ethnic cleanser . . . homophobic, racist . . . malevolent bully . . . psychotic delinquent . . . the monster of the Bible"—he fixates on those particularly abhorrent depictions of the Deity that rightly deserve to be shelved, while failing to mention that the Bible contains many more genial and even noble portrayals of God.[3]

It is also a common offense among those who are 'agenda-driven' that they 'cherry-pick' biblical texts to support a preconceived thesis. One familiar form of fundamentalism defines the biblical God as an almighty, omniscient, male, and highly selective source of salvation, while the neo-atheists rely on a selection of proof-texts consistent with the loathsome God they wish to portray. Both ignore the obvious and vital fact that *the Bible contains the breadth and complexity of human responses to a Be-ing that must forever remain beyond the creative comprehension of the human mind.*

Classical theology has understood and clearly articulated this. The Christian apophatic tradition, or *via negativa,* that found expression in the writings of Thomas Aquinas (1225–1274), Meister Eckhart (1260–1327) and St John of the Cross (1542–1591) emphasised that "God is unknowable in Godself" and refused to restrict Godhood to human formularies and descriptions. "God as God in Godself is an unsearchable mystery," they would insist; or, as Peter Carnley echoing Saint Paul neatly expresses it, "the object of our religious conviction can only ever be perceived dimly, like reflections in glass".[4] To be sure, one can find hints of an apophatic tradition in the Bible (e.g. Exodus 3; Isa 55:8; Rom 11:33) but sophisticated theological reflection did not appear until many centuries *after* the biblical texts.

The Hebraic God was initially an anthropomorphic conception, and was intimately involved in the historical lives and events of a particular nation and its citizens. And thus, since the ideational process operated by appropriating human or natural categories, Yahweh could be assigned such varied metaphors as rock, wind, fire, tent, temple, cloud, king, judge, shepherd, etc. The feminist theologian, Dorothee Sölle, makes the valid point that most of the biblical images of God were "andromorphic" rather than simply anthropomorphic, and thus presumed "the usual identification of human being with the male!"[5] Indeed, it must be admitted that female images of the divine were generally viewed negatively by both Jews and Christians, although a few did somehow find their way into the biblical texts (e.g. Hos 11:3–4; Isa 66:13; Matt 23:37/Luke 13:34). In short, modern scholars almost universally agree that the Bible is a human document that "belongs in the historical sphere [and] speaks from historical people to historical people".[6]

At the same time they also acknowledge that the Scriptures contain a number of ideas that, in the light of present-day knowledge and worldviews, are not only obsolete but morally repugnant. As John Shelby Spong has shown in *The Sins of Scripture*, the Bible includes texts that have been used to justify the oppression or degradation of women, children, sexual minorities, and even our planetary environment. This observation is not intended to impugn the value or status of the Scriptures, but to highlight the importance of examining them critically and using the best and most recent historical, cultural and linguistic tools. Indeed, at the heart of this methodology is an insistence on taking the Bible *seriously* as the *sacred* stories of "a God-infused humanity".[7]

The Bible bears witness to people who throughout history have expressed their deepest hopes and fears as they live out their lives in the belief that there is a God who loves and cares for them. The key to understanding what biblical authors say about

God is to uncover the historical context in which they lived or the particular personal situation that contributes to their spiritual search and pleas for divine assistance.

The Bible is a holy book because it abounds in thoughtful people's ideas about the nature of Holiness. It must be read with an appreciation of what form critics call *Sitz im Leben*—the setting in the life of the people. What was the original context in which the story, psalm, parable, song, etc., was composed? What meaning was the original speaker/writer trying to convey? How do we interpret their context and theological explanation today? By asking these questions we soon realize that the Bible is not inerrant or internally consistent in all its parts. We have to decide which of their insights are so culturally and historically fossilized that they are now obsolete, and which remain pearls of such great price that they continue to reveal a God that we can find relevant to worship today.

Human Words about Jesus
Become Words about a Divine Jesus

Similarly, it must be admitted that the New Testament consists of human words about Jesus. It seems an obvious assertion, but one that is surprisingly often overlooked by Christian commentators. The writers of the first and second centuries used the cultural, religious, social, and linguistic formulas of their contemporary world both in asking and responding to the question attributed to Jesus by the author of Mark's Gospel: "Who do you say that I am?" (Mark 8:38).

The labels and titles ascribed to Jesus by early Christians—Son of Man, Son of God, Son of David, Christ, Lord, Rabbi, Prophet, Logos, etc.—were taken directly from the Jewish, Roman, or Greek cultural worlds that informed their authors. These nomenclatures did not drop from the sky but represent current concepts of the time that could readily be reapplied to Jesus. Whether Jesus himself would have approved of many, some, or none of these designations is beyond the scope of this chapter; but that question has generated much debate among New Testament scholars.[8] What is not in dispute is that within a generation or two of his death, his followers began to talk about Jesus in lofty terms, and that two or three decades later the man Jesus had achieved an exalted status. Two examples will suffice to show this Christological development.

The first appears in Paul's letter to the Philippians. It is almost unanimously agreed by New Testament scholars that a pre-Pauline hymn of praise to Jesus circulated within early Christianity. Although its date of composition is uncertain it is probable that what we find in Phil 2:6–11 was originally in circulation within a decade or so after the crucifixion of Jesus:[9]

> who, though he was in the form of God,
> did not regard equality with God
> as something to be exploited,
> but emptied himself,
> taking the form of a slave,
> being born in human likeness.
> And being found in human form,
> he humbled himself
> and became obedient to the point of death
> —even death on a cross:
> Therefore God also highly exalted him
> and gave him the name
> that is above every name,
> so that at the name of Jesus
> every knee should bend,
> in heaven and on earth and under the earth,
> and every tongue should confess
> that Jesus Christ is Lord,
> to the glory of God the Father.

What this song of praise demonstrates is that very soon after Jesus' death Christians had begun to transfer the language usually associated with God to the person of Jesus. Christology and theology become closely intertwined. Indeed, we can safely accept Stephen Patterson's assertion that "whenever Jesus is the subject, someone . . . is thinking about God".[10] To be sure, academics continue to haggle over what the hymn proclaims about the *exact* nature of Jesus' lordship and the degree of his exaltation. It would seem that Jesus has not yet been elevated to the Council of Nicea's (325 CE) understanding of the second person of the Trinity, but it is fair to say that his new status places him in a special category of humanity. Perhaps this judicious assessment from Karen Armstrong captures what is being expressed:

> The careful wording of the hymn made it clear that there was a distinction between *kyrios* and God. Even though Paul and the evangelists all called Jesus the 'son of God' they were not making divine claims for him. They would have been quite shocked by this idea. For Jews, a 'son of God' was a perfectly normal human being who had been *raised to special intimacy with God and had been given a divine mandate.*[11]

The second example appears repeatedly and in various forms in the earliest of the Gospels. During Jesus' baptism a voice from heaven proclaims him "my Son, the Beloved" (Mark 1:11), and upon his death it is recorded that a Roman soldier exclaims, "Truly this man was God's son" (Mark 15:39). Again, this may stop a bit short of the Nicean formulation, but the claim to being elevated to some sort of special status is beyond question.

The key point to note here is that Jesus' followers were now openly expressing their belief "in a cultic deity . . . a kind of anti-god to the Roman state gods".[12] The Roman historian Pliny may tell his Emperor that this is merely a "perverse and extravagant superstition", but Christians have raised the stakes by worshipping Jesus as "the Christ", and thus making him, in effect, a non-sanctioned Roman god. However, they would have to wait a few hundred years before their Jesus became the official object of devotion throughout the Roman Empire.

To sum up, the earliest Christian faith communities responded *theologically* to the sayings and acts of Jesus. Jesus-talk became God-talk, as Patterson neatly explains:

> Those earliest Christians claimed that in his words and deeds they had come to know who God really is, what God is really like. Why? Simply because they had experienced Jesus that way. They heard Jesus' words and risked calling them the Word of God because they chose to believe in the kind of God they saw in him. Their responses of faith did not replace what Jesus had said and done with something new. Rather, they elevated what they had experienced in Jesus to a new kind of status: a claim about who God is, a theological claim.[13]

God-Talk in the Bible

Thus far I have indicated that God-talk permeates the Bible; it is now time to present what must be an obvious corollary to that statement: the Bible cannot be understood without some appreciation of its theological biases. For without a reasonably clear understanding of the God (or gods) it portrays, the Bible becomes spiritually hollow, little more than a sometimes-fascinating socio-historical account of Jewish and Christian communities. To remove theology from the Bible is to exclude one of its primary concerns and to interpret it as a non-faith document. On the contrary, the Bible is a source book for theology.

This does not mean that the Bible is a theological textbook, a mother lode to be mined for doctrinal truth, but that it contains a good deal of what we today might call theological reflection. James Barr explains this by neatly discriminating between overt theological statements and implied theology:

> A distinction has to be made between *overt* theological statement and *implied* or *underlying* theology. Overt theological statement, in the form of considered and formulated doctrine occupies only

a fairly limited area in the Bible. Much larger areas are taken up by presentation in narrative form, poetic form etc. It is perfectly proper to speak about the 'theology' of this narrative or poetic literature, thus the theology of St Mark, the theology of the P document, or the theology of a group of Psalms; but this theology is normally not overtly declared or formulated; it is conveyed indirectly through the selection and emphasis of material in historical narrative or poetic composition.[14]

It is to that *implied or underlying* theology of the New Testament, and in particular the theological outlook of the central figure of Christianity, Jesus of Nazareth, that I now turn my attention.

From Jesus to God, Not Vice-Versa!

What was Jesus' understanding of God? Who was the God of Jesus? What was Jesus' theology? Patterson correctly notes that New Testament scholars rarely ask these questions because they are more interested in uncovering clues as to who the historical Jesus might have been.[15] Moreover, scholars have long confused Christology with theology, attempting to discover whether Jesus considered himself to be God or was personally aware of what has often been referred to as his "messianic consciousness." Even such a radical theologian as John Hick is guilty of straining the biblical text to breaking point in this flowery and unsubstantiated interpretation of the personal state of Jesus' consciousness:

> The most intense and continuous such awareness [of the presence of God] known to us in the Christian tradition is that of Jesus himself. He seems to have been conscious all the time of the presence of God as the most real of all realities. God, the heavenly Father to whom he spoke in prayer, in whose name he healed and pronounced forgiveness, and about whom he taught, was as real to him as the people he was talking to, or as the hills and Lake of Galilee. . . . In other words, he seems to have lived more or less continuously on the heights of religious awareness.[16]

That particular approach to what Jesus was thinking has proved to be futile, since it is now all but universally conceded that a biblical text cannot return us to the inner workings of the author's mind, let alone provide entry into the conscious or unconscious thoughts of Jesus. The relativist hermeneutic tradition based upon the writings of philosophers Martin Heidegger (1889–1976), Hans Georg Gadamer (1900–2002) and Paul Ricoeur (1913–2005) has persuasively demolished the notion that we can 'get into the head' of an author (*psychologism*) and somehow unlock his or her original intention. On the contrary, we can never escape from the hermeneutical circle of continually interpreting and reinterpreting texts. Interpretation is never without presuppositions, and is always "relative to the particular and contingent 'location' of the interpreter". The essential function of written language is not to reveal the "inner experience" of the author or her subject, but to let us know "what the author is saying about some important subject matter".[17] The only way to discover Jesus' theology, therefore, is to search the records of what he said and did for clues to the God he believed in—and what is perhaps more important, the God he wanted *us* to believe in.

Jesus' theology is thus inseparable from the historical Jesus, since the portrait of Jesus that historical scholars have assembled is our only source of information about the God of Jesus. It seems an obvious point, but all too many Christian academics somehow overlook it. Instead of commencing with Jesus and deriving pertinent observations about the God he seems to have been proclaiming, they begin from their idea of God and try to apply it to Jesus. N. T. Wright expresses the point succinctly:

> History is necessary when we look at Jesus because faith itself demands it. . . . [If Jesus] really was fully human, . . . if we take that [statement] seriously, we cannot shirk the historical task. We are promised that when we look at [the Gospel of] John or [the epistles of] Paul or [the letter to the] Hebrews, that is when

we see Jesus more clearly—as the human being he was—and we discover what the word 'God' actually means. Classic Christology does not assume a meaning for God and then fit Jesus into that. It looks long and lovingly at Jesus and then says we need to rethink what we mean by God around that fixed point.[18]

In short, if we proclaim God was in Jesus then unless we know who Jesus was, we might have God wrong! We must start with Jesus and then define who God is, not fit Jesus into the God we believe in!

Jesus' Theology

It is accepted by most New Testament scholars that Jesus' central proclamation concerned the kingdom/empire/realm of God.[19] However, since the publication of Albert Schweitzer's magnum opus *The Quest of the Historical Jesus* (1906), the issue of whether it was to be a *future* or *present* empire has become one of the most hotly disputed topics in New Testament studies. The discussion centers on whether Jesus was either an apocalyptic/eschatological prophet who thought that upon his death the end of the world and the arrival of God's empire would shortly follow (Schweitzer's own view); or whether he was a wisdom teacher who came to call for the establishment of a new and radically inclusive community. This is not some arcane academic argument. It not only goes to the heart of who Jesus was and the nature of the God he proclaimed, but is crucial in deciding "what sort of religion Christianity is".[20]

I side with those scholars who argue for a sapiential Jesus who announced that God's empire was to be made real *now* by those who accepted his teaching. It was to be experienced as a present reality by those first disciples and to be similarly practiced by subsequent generations. Jesus' theology was thus not dominated by the expectation of an imminent and cataclysmic intervention by God in history, but rather down-to-earth, everyday advice on how God's empire was to be created here on earth. In his unique teaching method of parables and aphorisms, Jesus was a social revolutionary who founded a short-lived 'egalitarian' community based upon a 'discipleship of equals' that broke down barriers of race, class, gender and ethnicity.[21]

The parables, widely hailed as "the distinctive voice of Jesus", depict an alternative society in which "the empire of God brings everyone to the same level." The empire of God was in direct contrast to the officially sanctioned empire of Rome, which included the Temple authorities who colluded with their occupying overlords. Jesus challenged the confiscatory dictatorship of Rome as well as its infiltration and domination of the Jewish Temple.

As a popularly proclaimed rabbi, Jesus advocated an alternative "counter-world", a "shared egalitarianism of spiritual and material resources" that clearly challenged Roman political, economic, and religious domination. This advocacy of "living in relationships of mutual care" is reflected in the ecclesial utopian community portrayed in Acts 4:32–35.[22] Of course, the mere advocacy of such a spiritual and social program by a Mediterranean peasant would have been viewed as seditious by the Roman authorities, and it could lead to only one outcome: arrest for treason, followed by crucifixion.

It was his proclamation of this alternative vision and this subversive empire that brought Jesus to the attention of the Roman authorities. And contrary to the Gospel writers' portrayal of his humane and judicious rule, Pontius Pilate was in fact a brutal Roman prefect who "unleashed a reign of terror" from 26–36 CE. He had no qualms about ordering the crucifixion of a suspected malefactor on the flimsiest of evidence, and he would surely have dealt with a peasant from Nazareth who proclaimed a rival empire in summary fashion.[23]

Significantly, Jesus' message and program of radical inclusivity was *based on his ideas of God*. Charles Hedrick connects Jesus' theology to his program and to his death in a single concise paragraph:

He believed in God and found in his personal faith a sense of authority for his public acts and discourse. He believed God was working through him to reclaim complete control of human affairs. When fully realized, God's imperial rule would bring about a reversal of human values and overhaul the structures of society. Quite predictably, therefore, Jesus found his natural place among the poor and irreverent on the margins of society, rather than in its main stream. The 'righteous' and the religious authorities were particularly subject to his scathing wit and censure. Likely the reversal of values he announced and its implied challenge to the power structures of human society brought about his death. The fact that he was killed by an official act of the governing authority suggests that his public career was viewed, in some sense, as a serious threat to public welfare.[24]

So, who exactly is the God of Jesus?

Patterson focuses the issue by asking two crucial questions: "What is the character of God that comes to expression in Jesus' words and deeds? What did Jesus believe to be true about God that led him to speak of God's empire in the way that he did?"[25] Clearly, the answers we give to these questions will determine not only the kind of God that we believe in, but the type of Christianity that we seek to advance today.

First, Patterson argues, Jesus' words and deeds reflected a belief that "God is not remote but directly involved in the lives of ordinary people". God is known in the midst of life, can be addressed intimately, and welcomes *all* into his family. There are no outsiders, no expendables, and no one is unclean. Further, "the experience of God is transformative and leads to new acts of love directed towards others". Thus, "God calls persons into relationships of radical love and mutual care".

Second, Jesus' words and deeds manifested an inclusive God who invites us to "form communities in which the experience of love and care would be institutionalised"—where, in the words of a modern hymn "people matter, people count".[26] This is the empire of God. Patterson concludes his disquisition with this insightful observation:

> What people experienced in Jesus was a word of love, acceptance, belonging, and value. Jesus spoke about God in just these terms. So when people heard his words and believed them to be true, their experience became not just that of a remarkable teacher. They experienced his words as the Word of God. This was the beginning of the Christian understanding of who God is. It began with the theology of Jesus himself.[27]

It is from this understanding of Jesus' theology that Christians proclaim their faith. In short, Jesus' understanding of God is the God in whom we also believe.

Christianity Today: Why What We Say about Jesus' God Matters

In *Religion Under Attack* (2011), I argued that contemporary Christianity must, if it is to survive the challenges of scientists, the attacks of the new atheists, the spirituality revolution, and mass defection by unbelievers, develop an inclusive theology and break free from the dogmatism and exclusivity that characterizes its conservative elements. I now further contend that such a theology offers an accurate and compelling representation of the God of Jesus that I have outlined in this chapter.

The revolutionary concept of an egalitarian community that proclaims the all-embracing love of a compassionate God has been hijacked by those whose outmoded fundamentalist religion is correctly ridiculed by intelligent atheists as "violent, irrational, intolerant, allied to racism, tribalism, and bigotry, invested in ignorance and hostile to free inquiry, contemptuous of women and coercive toward children".[28] It is time for ordinary Christians not only to raise their voices in outraged reply: "That's not my religion and that's not the God that Jesus preached", but also to expound the God of Jesus in their communities of faith and in the wider world.

The God of Jesus must be called upon to inform the contemporary Christian community of its commitment to a new 'empire' that breaks down the barriers of gender, class, patriarchy, and race. This is still the revolutionary message of Jesus, whose spiritual and social program was to create communities embodying that vision. Indeed, as Marcus Borg reminds us, the ideal of a loving, inclusive community is at the core of the biblical narrative:

> Community is utterly central in the Hebrew Bible and early Christianity. An individualistic spirituality is quite foreign to the biblical vision of life with God. In its worship and practices, the community celebrates life with God, nourishes and mediates the new way of being, and embodies the egalitarian social vision running through the Bible from exodus through the Jesus movement and evident in early Christianity. Christian life in community is meant to create an alternative world, a counter-world, to the world of normalcy and domination.[29]

The role and mission of the Christian community is to live up to that vision of a transformed world in the name of the God that Jesus came to proclaim.

Conclusion

In this chapter I have argued the Bible is not a theological textbook but a religious anthology that contains a broad sampling of how ancient writers thought about God. God-talk permeates its texts, but they do not present a consistent theology. As early as 1860 the Anglican theologian Benjamin Jowett recognised that the Bible "is to be interpreted like other books, with attention to the character of its authors, and the prevailing state of civilization and knowledge, with allowance for peculiarities in style and language, and modes of thought and figure of speech".[30] Today we must broaden that advice by undertaking a critical examination of the theological biases of its writers and the reasons for their particular understandings of God. This is not to denigrate their search for the divine, but to read the texts with eyes wide open to the historical, social and cultural factors that influenced them.

It has been my central concern to show how New Testament writers adapted the God-talk of the Hebrew Bible to their attempts to explain their understanding of Jesus. In particular, I have contended that rather than impose *our* ideas of God upon Jesus, we must begin the search for God with the historical Jesus. This is what later Christian writers articulated by the doctrine of Incarnation: namely, that God comes to us in the midst of human existence and is revealed in a specific human person, a figure of history.

The God of Jesus is thus rooted in the historical person from Nazareth who preached a message of radical inclusivity that has consequences for the way Christians live two thousand years later. We must continue that social and religious program in *ecclesias*—church communities that mirror the empire of God—because, as Patterson observes, that is what Jesus demands of us:

> Jesus challenged those around him to re-create the world, to re-construct human life and relationships in a way that would reflect and embody that ultimate reality. That is what the empire of God is, or would be, if one were to choose to risk it.[31]

Notes

1. The inclusion in the Bible of the books of the Apocrypha has proved problematic for some churches.

2. Hedrick, *When Faith Meets Reason*, xiii.

3. Dawkins, *The God Delusion*, 31, 38, 45.

4. Carnley, *Reflections in Glass*, 29.

5. Sölle, *Theology for Skeptics*, 34n1.

6. Sölle, *Thinking About God*, 24–25.

7. Spong, *The Sins of Scripture*, 298.

8. For a fascinating and well-balanced debate on this matter featuring a liberal and a conservative Christian, see Borg and Wright, *The Meaning of Jesus*.

9. The notable exception to this academic consensus is Fee, *Paul's Letter to the Philippians*. Fee argues that no corresponding Jewish hymn of praise can be found in Hebrew psalmody, and thus it must have originated with Paul himself.

10. Patterson, *The God of Jesus*, 44.

11. Armstrong, *The Battle for God*, 88–89.

12. Thiessen and Merz, *The Historical Jesus*, 81.

13. Patterson, *The God of Jesus*, 47.

14. Barr, *The Bible in the Modern World*, 90. "P" is short for Priestly: one of several sources of the Hebrew Bible texts.

15. Patterson, *The God of Jesus*, 112. This section is heavily influenced by Patterson's interweaving of the quest of the historical Jesus and Jesus' theology.

16. Goulder and Hick, *Why Believe in God?*, 38.

17. Westphal, *Whose Community?*, 34.

18. Transcript of a lecture in Sydney presented by N .T. Wright on "The Historical Jesus", March 15, 2006, at the Christian Studies Institute, Macquarie University, Sydney. This can be viewed at http://www.youtube.com/watch?v=VrzjzFppxAg&feature=related.

19. 'Realm' and 'empire' are now widely used to avoid the sexist overtones of kingdom. In this chapter I shall follow the Jesus Seminar in using 'empire'.

20. Patterson in Miller, *The Apocalyptic Jesus*, 163. This will be explored further in my forthcoming book, *Which Jesus? Whose Christ?*

21. Elisabeth Schüssler Fiorenza coined the phrase 'discipleship of equals'. John Dominic Crossan, Gerd Theissen and many Fellows of the Jesus Seminar view Jesus as a social revolutionary.

22. I have here summarised the ideas of Bernard Brandon Scott, "The Reappearance of Parables", and John Dominic Crossan, "Jesus as a Mediterranean Jewish Peasant", in Hoover, *Profiles of Jesus*: 19–40 and 161–68, respectively. Scott and Crossan differ slightly in that Scott argues that Jesus primarily presented a vision or "glimpsed alternative", whereas Crossan believes that Jesus had both an alternative vision *and* a concrete social program.

23. Verhoeven, *Jesus of Nazareth*, 26.

24. Hedrick, "Jesus of Nazareth", in Hoover, *Profiles of Jesus*, 71.

25. Patterson, *The God of Jesus*, 113.

26. "Sing We of a Modern City" (1968) by Frederik Hermanus Kaan (1929–2009).

27. Patterson, *The God of Jesus*, 118.

28. Hitchens, *God Is Not Great*, 56.

29. Borg in Miller, *The Apocalyptic Jesus*, 156.
30. Jowett, *Essays and Reviews*, 517.
31. Patterson, *The God of Jesus*, 162.

5

Scripture and Formation for Ministry

Susan Crothers-Robertson

We are formed to be emptied of ourselves, to allow room for God to work in and on us; we are formed to serve others with all that we have; we are formed for ministry, not for careers.

—Lizette Larson-Miller[1]

"Hear . . . Read, Mark, Learn and Inwardly Digest . . ."

The collect for the Second Sunday of Advent in the *Book of Common Prayer* of 1662 (BCP) famously seeks that the worshippers may be engaged so deeply with the Scriptures that they (we) are thoroughly transformed:

> Blessed Lord, who hast caused all holy Scriptures to be written for our learning: Grant that we may in such wise hear them, read, mark, learn, and inwardly digest them, that by patience, and comfort of thy holy Word, we may embrace, and ever hold fast, the blessed hope of everlasting life, which thou hast given us in our Saviour Jesus Christ. Amen.

The collect offers a series of verbs—action words. We are exhorted to do something (indeed, several things) about the Bible, and in the process of doing this combination of actions we seek formation—even transformation—for ministry. We can consider these sacred verbs in turn.

81

Hearing . . .

I sit amongst a cloud of witnesses in the beautiful sandstone Chapel of the Holy Spirit that stands at the heart of St Francis Theological College. It is a place where, for many years, theological students, those preparing for ordination, and staff have gathered to pray. If only these stones could speak, what stories of both joys and sorrows they would tell. We gather each morning, noon and night during term time to find something to quench our thirst. Morning after morning as we begin the day we long for the spiritual depth to help us move through the day. Then, as the day ends, we want to let go of all that has been and hopefully find a restful night.

It was there I sat, early in the academic year, as students prepared for Morning Prayer, like so many before them across the decades. Yet for some new students Morning Prayer is a foreign concept. The bell rang out, calling the community to worship. The candles were lit. The readings of the day were marked in the Bible. The student who led Morning Prayer processed in, wearing a new cassock and freshly starched surplice, and looking a little uncomfortable. When it came time for the Psalms to be read, there were awkward pauses as we once again tried to find our rhythm together. The reader walked to the lectern to read the Scriptures set for the day. But their voice was bland, the words read as little more than a news report. I wanted the reader to hear what they were saying, to feel it in the depth of their being. I wanted them to help the Scriptures come alive for us as hearers. Instead we got to the end and I thought, "Did we hear, know or believe what was just said? Did the reading make a difference?"

What does it mean to 'hear' and 'listen' to the Scriptures? There is no doubt we filter what we hear. All of us can fall into the trap of leaning a little too heavily on our knowledge. How do we let go of our so-called knowledge and really 'hear' and 'listen' to the Scriptures as they are read? When we first hear we may let it settle on the surface of our lives, but then in the ebb and flow of daily life—as we mull over what has been said—there is the dance of the living Word that calls us into action, confronts us, and draws us out of our settled lives; beckoning us to respond.

We come with knowledge and may even think we know all there is to know about a particular passage. Yet we are invited to let go of all we know and 'attend' to the Scriptures. As we wrestle with what we are hearing, we are both challenged and affirmed. But this can only happen if we let go, actively listen, and hear. When we do this we find that we actually do not know it all and we 'hear' (discern) for the first time. This is when God's wisdom awakens something deep within.

Read . . .

Candidates come into college with a variety of experiences in reading the Bible. Some have been heavily involved in their parish communities as readers, teaching Sunday School, preaching, leading Bible studies, or practicing *lectio divina*, while others may have had very little if any experience of engaging with the Bible in these ways. All will have been members of faith communities where the collective reading of the Bible is a primary spiritual practice, and all will have some appreciation of the imperative to read the Scriptures—publicly and privately, individually and collectively. As candidates engage in theological studies and ministry formation, they find the Scriptures are taken seriously but not necessarily literally,[2] the Scriptures are 'criticized' and yet preached, they are both deconstructed and used in prayer.

The 'daily offices' of Morning Prayer and Evening Prayer are a vital part of our spirituality. Yet they are something that many of the candidates find a challenge. So often they start off the academic year 'doing' the daily offices because it is expected of them. As the year unfolds there is a noticeable change. The rhythm of the offices becomes part of their life. They become aware there is something so much bigger than a person praying.

They come to realize that all over the world there are others praying the daily offices and we are part of a larger community that transcends place and time. In the gathering of the 'two or three' the risen One is among us, and God's presence transforms us.

Integral to the daily office is saying the Psalms together—or should I say, praying the Psalms? Our lectionary for the daily offices provides for the complete Psalter—all 150 Psalms— to be read over and over in our worship. Several times a year the cycle recurs. Each time we pray the offices we are immersed once again in the language, in the faith, in the hopes and fears of the people of God. Their words become our words, generating our personal and collective religious lexicon.

We read both Psalms and selected lectionary texts together with others when that is possible, and privately when it is not possible to gather with others. As 'people of the Book', we read, we read and we read. As we read we are shaped and formed. The story recited in the Psalms and proclaimed in the lectionary readings becomes our story. The faith of Abraham and Sarah forms *our* faith, the God of Moses and Miriam becomes *our* God.

Mark . . .

This verb within the BCP collect encourages us to engage with the Scriptures using our minds: to 'mark' them! Anyone who 'marks' the Scriptures will be thinking about the content, making connections, noting intertextual links within the canon and beyond its boundaries, drawing on our wider knowledge of life in this world gifted to us by the arts and sciences of our human cultures.

In all these 'markings', our candidates are thinking critically; taking the Bible seriously, even if not literally. If they can learn this life-giving skill in their academic life, they can harness it for their everyday life. It is in thinking critically that "they will be self-actualizing and self-determining".[3] Thinking critically not only impacts on how we read and engage with the Scriptures, but also helps us "to identify and challenge assumptions [we] bring to the study of any given text, situation, event or relationship".[4] I believe these are the critical skills needed by all in ministry.

I am often caught by surprise—even shocked—by how some students interpret the Scriptures. It is strange that some aspects of their lives, and their belief systems, have grown and matured as they have, while others seem not to have matured. For instance, they no longer believe in the tooth fairy, or Santa Claus or the Easter bunny. Yet when it comes to the Scriptures they often interpret them in a certain literal, fixed and rigid way. It seems they find it difficult to move beyond a Sunday School faith. Martin Percy suggests,

> Just as the doing of theology is a skill that must be learned if one is to progress from a childish faith to a mature faith, so people must be taught to read the Bible with mature theological lenses.[5]

Our role is to ensure that the candidate has exposure to and engagement with various forms of biblical scholarship. In engaging critically with biblical and theological scholarship, they can put away their immature belief systems and develop critical thinking that will result in a maturity of faith.

So while critical thinking is often baulked at, it is essential that candidates are equipped to embrace critical thinking instinctively. By using this skill when reading and 'marking' the Scriptures, their knowledge can be broadened to the point of being aware that others may interpret these sacred texts differently.[6] However, the point is not to understand or tame the Scriptures so that they become a worthless document that affirms what we already know and believe. Rather, it awakens the candidates to the realization that the way they interpret the Bible shapes *their* identity and how *they* do ministry. Students enter college with long-held beliefs about the nature and meaning of the Scriptures. Critical thinking confronts those beliefs, moving them from an unquestioning, naive and almost sentimental faith.

As their imaginations are opened, they become people with a living, critical faith. Their way of being is transformed.[7]

Learn . . .

One challenge we must face is that the Scriptures can be over-analysed. Walter Brueggemann suggests that the Scriptures' "playfulness, openness, and ambiguity (are) consequently made to yield to a scholastic pattern of conclusions that make the text almost too predictable and familiar to bother with".[8] There is a very real possibility of getting to the point of saying, "Well, why bother?"

Richard Briggs expresses a concern that we may have gone too far with biblical criticism:

> the critical impulse once unleashed has proved to be a voracious beast, and seems inevitably to push the epistemological bar higher and higher. How do we know? How can we be sure? Have we read enough possible parallel texts yet to understand the literary trope in view or the historical claim being made? And it needs to be considered whether, or in what sense, Christian formation is served by such agendas.[9]

James Packer is quite sure that biblical criticism has gone too far! He believes that "unbelief of the Bible is now at a premium" in theological seminaries and continues:

> In the seminaries, alas, there is a habit encouraging the way-out, enterprising thinkers who follow this track of leaving the Bible behind, and developing their own theologies in the way that learned people have been doing all through the nineteenth and twentieth centuries. . . . Persons who get sent to theological teaching institutions where this is happening have their minds stuffed with this kind of theologizing and then, just like school-masters, they go out and teach what they were taught.[10]

Packer goes so far as to say that teaching critical thinking and encouraging people to pay attention to the diversity within the Scriptures is a serious violation of Article 20:

You do not need to tell me that the violation of this Article is
one of the besetting sins of theological leaders today both in the
Anglican Church and in other churches.[11]

This seems to me to be scaremongering. To think critically,
and to engage deeply with the text as it actually exists with all its
human diversity and inconsistencies, may indeed challenge our
Christian identity. Yes, a central part of our belief is being questioned, but not for us to lose faith. Our faith is not dissolved;
on the contrary, we are learning to question in order to build
substance and durability.

While some question whether biblical criticism has gone
too far, from a feminist point of view, biblical criticism has not
gone far enough. How are we—as Schüssler Fiorenza asks—to
take the Bible into the 'public square' if we do not first read it
critically, being aware of the words of abuse and discrimination?
Those training for ordination and who have benefited from biblical criticism in their own studies have a responsibility to reveal
how the Scriptures have been used to oppress and harm in the
name of God. This injustice is not just from the past but exists
also in our present. The Scriptures continue to be used to oppress and exclude anyone who appears to live 'differently'.

The challenge is to come to the Scriptures with 'eyes wide
open', or at least being aware of the context from which we interpret the Scriptures. How can we reinterpret, re-imagine, and
re-cast the story, opening minds and hearts to the ambiguity that
is offered within.

Certainly, one element of practical wisdom that comes with critical thinking that is mindful and aware is the ongoing experience
of wonder. The ability to be awed, excited, and inspired by ideas
is a practice that radically opens the mind.[12]

Biblical criticism alerts us to the knowledge that the sacred
text can be read and understood on so many different levels.
The Scriptures have the potential to harm, as people use them to
dominate and wield power, but that does not mean we disregard

them. Indeed, it is through biblical criticism that we become aware of the many voices that birthed the Scriptures into being and come to speak in our time and place.

St Francis of Assisi, the patron saint of our College, once said these words to Brother Anthony of Padua, who was about to begin teaching the brothers:

> It pleases me that you teach sacred theology to the brothers, as long as—in the words of the Rule—you 'do not extinguish the spirit of prayer and devotion' with study of this kind.[13]

We do run a risk with biblical criticism that the spirit of prayer and devotion might be extinguished. Yet, as St Francis said, 'sacred theology' is a good thing. Elizabeth Schüssler Fiorenza goes further as she counsels us to adopt a critical stance even to the Scriptures:

> In order to foster the ability of spiritual discernment, cultural and religious education needs to enable readers to take a critical stance toward all human words, especially to those that claim the unmediated power and authority.[14]

By engaging with current biblical scholarship there is an opportunity to realize that there is more to the Scriptures than previously known. Critical thinking enables us to create scaffolding within which to build our identity as Christians. As readers of Scripture we have a responsibility as agents and expressions of the living Word. What a responsibility that is!

Inwardly Digest . . .

One wonders whether the Scriptures continue to inspire those who are preparing for ordination? Are the Scriptures a place where candidates encounter the living Word, where they find life-giving stories that enable them to be equipped for a life of ministry? Does their encounter with the living Word create a response that leads them "to right living, to conduct of justice and peace in communal, as well as personal life"?[15] If the students genuinely believe that the word being spoken has the potential to inspire and move them into action, then surely there would be an urgency to respond.

The Bible does not speak with one voice, but as Martyn Percy suggests, "many voices symphonic in character—a restless and inspiring chorus of testaments, whose authority rests upon its very plurality".[16] While there are many voices, surely there are common goals that call us into action. We are called to bring peace where there is bloodshed, to bring unity where there is disunity, to bring inclusiveness where others are excluded, and a richness where there is poverty. As 'people of the Book' we are to take such action, and rejoice in the rich diversity of the many voices found within the Scriptures.

Balancing Scripture, reason and tradition is a sensitive yet necessary art for people of faith generally, as well as those preparing for ordination. This triad is not exclusive to the Anglican tradition.[17] Rather, many Christian traditions use a similar formula giving varying weight to each category. William Marshall believes that invoking Scripture, reason and tradition allows for flexibility.[18] The Bible does not stand alone, but is informed by "the assumptions, thought-forms, worldview, culture, and especially the community, of the readers".[19] The Reformers fought for the Bible to be written in the language of the people, so it could be not only 'heard' but also 'inwardly digested'.

The Scriptures and Anglican Identity

The *Thirty-Nine Articles of Religion* have a particular place within some (but not all) expressions of the Anglican tradition. They have never been part of the Scottish Episcopal Church tradition and do not play the same role within the Episcopal Church in the USA as they do in England or Australia. In Muriel Porter's words, they

> are a product of compromise, arising from a politically-fraught sixteenth-century process whereby the Church of England, under

Queen Elizabeth I, set down its view in relation to the theological controversies of the time.[20]

While their historical origins are complex and their status sometimes controversial, the *Articles* have informed Anglican attitudes to the Bible in many parts of the world.[21] For instance, Article Six includes the affirmation that "Holy Scripture containeth all things necessary to salvation". The Anglican Reformers believed that the Scriptures were an essential *and sufficient* basis for Christian faith. These words are echoed in the ordination service for priesthood where each candidate is asked,

> Are you convinced that the Holy Scriptures contain all doctrine necessary for eternal salvation through faith in Jesus Christ, and are you determined to instruct from these Scriptures the people committed to your care, teaching nothing as essential to salvation which cannot be demonstrated from the Scriptures?[22]

As Alan Bartlett says, "Scripture is reaffirmed in the Lambeth Quadrilateral, as the first of Anglicanism's non-negotiables, and in the Declaration of Assent as the place of unique revelation."[23] The centrality of reading of the Scriptures in public liturgies, and in the vernacular, has been a crucial part of church practice from the Reformation until today. The Scriptures are meant to be easily accessible to all people, not just the elite. While the Scriptures are central to our worship this does not make them "infallible",[24] but rather they are open to criticism, interpretation, and discussion.

Yet, the Bible does not stand alone, independent of its context. As Nicola Slee suggests, we are "marked" by both our history and by our contemporary interpretation of Scriptures.[25] Within many Christian traditions we read the Scriptures in a disciplined way, using a lectionary to inform us of what we are to read. By using the lectionary we read the Scriptures in a systematic way, so that within a three year cycle, we have 'heard, . . . read, marked, learned and inwardly digested' a large proportion of the Bible.

This means we do not pick and choose what we 'feel like' reading or preaching upon in some haphazard way. Rather, we are challenged and disciplined by a more holistic approach, formed with our sisters and brothers in the wider church, bringing us together as one, which is the 'relatedness' that Percy talks about.[26]

Like all Christians, we "read, mark, learn and inwardly digest" the Scriptures for wisdom on how to live our lives, who we are to be in the world, finding God, finding a way to live our faith and searching for meaning for our lives as Christians. Tradition and reason inform how we read the Bible critically, making us aware that there is no "absolute identification between the Bible and the word of God, recognizing rather that the Bible testifies to the word".[27] The tradition in which we were formed will impact on how we read and digest the Scriptures, which in turn will lead us to more than mere words on paper; it leads us to the Living Word. We allow God's Spirit to inspire us from the past, for the present that moves us into the future, beckoning us to new places we are yet to imagine.

Hearing, Once More . . .

We come to the end of the academic year. Once again, I am sitting in the college chapel. This time I sit in anticipation. There is gentle buzz of expectation in the air as the students prayerfully prepare for Morning Prayer. The readings of the day are marked in the large lectern Bible. The person who will be leading the office is also at the front finishing her preparations. The bell rings out, calling us to worship; a time-honoured tradition that expresses our identity is being enacted as we gather as a community. We are a community of learners who come to this chapel to 'hear, read, mark, learn and inwardly digest' the portion of Holy Scripture set for this day.

The person leading Morning Prayer opens up our time of worship with ancient words that have been said for centuries, linking us to the past. We move seamlessly into praying the Psalms together. It is like poetry and music to my ears. It comes time for the Bible reading. The person moves up to the lectern slowly and deliberately. As they are read, the words come alive with the potential to either affirm or transform.

We listen with anticipation, for we know that these ancient words can serve the gracious purposes of the Spirit who has new things to say to the churches. The leader prays: "May your word live in us." We complete the collective prayer with our response: "and bear much fruit for your glory!"

Notes

1. Larson-Miller, "Seminary Chapel", 92.
2. See Borg, *Reading the Bible Again for the First Time.*
3. Hooks, *Teaching Critical Thinking*, 183.
4. Foster et al., *Educating Clergy*, 92.
5. Martin, *Pedagogy on the Bible*, 74.
6. Hooks, *Teaching Critical Thinking*, 10.
7. Foster et al., *Educating Clergy*, 102.
8. Brueggemann, *The Word That Redescribes the World*, 5.
9. Briggs, "Scripture in Christian Formation", 86.
10. Packer, "The Centrality of Holy Scripture", 45.
11. Packer, "The Centrality of Holy Scripture", 31.
12. Hooks, *Teaching Critical Thinking*, 187–88.
13. Armstrong and Brady, *Francis and Clare*, 79.
14. Schüssler Fiorenza, "Reading Scripture in the Context of Empire", 167.
15. Slee, "Word", 37.
16. Percy, Preface, in Porter, *Sydney Anglicans*, x.
17. Marshall, *Scripture, Tradition and Reason*, 12.
18. Marshall, *Scripture, Tradition and Reason*, 17.
19. Marshall, *Scripture, Tradition and Reason*, 19.
20. Porter, *Sydney Anglicans*, 23.
21. Interestingly within the Australian context the Thirty-Nine Articles continue to be produced with the Prayer Books. Australian clergy are expected to assent to the Thirty-Nine Articles, and they continue to appear in the constitution. English clergy only have to acknowledge them. (Porter, *Sydney Anglicans*, 23–24)

22. *A Prayer Book for Australia*, 794.

23. Bartlett, *Passionate Balance*, 91. The four matters that the Lambeth Conference of 1888 identified as essential in any pursuit of Christian unity are: "(a) The Holy Scriptures of the Old and New Testaments, as 'containing all things necessary to salvation', and as being the rule and ultimate standard of faith. (b) The Apostles' Creed, as the Baptismal Symbol; and the Nicene Creed, as the sufficient statement of the Christian faith. (c) The two Sacraments ordained by Christ Himself—Baptism and the Supper of the Lord— ministered with unfailing use of Christ's words of Institution, and of the elements ordained by Him. (d) The Historic Episcopate, locally adapted in the methods of its administration to the varying needs of the nations and peoples called of God into the Unity of His Church." Available online at http://anglicansonline.org/basics/ Chicago_Lambeth.html.

24. Chapman, *Means of Grace*, 41.

25. Slee, "Word", 42.

26. Percy, *Shaping the Church*, 12.

27. Slee, "Word", 42.

6

The Bible and Liturgy

Marian Free

On a Sunday towards the end of the church year, the Gospel set for the liturgy is Matt 25:14–30—commonly known as the Parable of the Talents. This parable occurs in two places in the New Testament: here in the Gospel of Matthew and in Luke 19:12–27. The two versions of the story are quite different. For example, the chief protagonist is identified as a nobleman in Luke, but not in Matthew. In Luke the nobleman goes to Rome to seek a kingdom for himself (which results in the citizens—who hate him—sending a delegation after him); in Matthew the man simply goes away.[1] Three slaves in Matthew compare with ten in Luke. The former are given responsibility for a huge amount of money, while the latter receive a large, but much smaller, amount. Luke's nobleman instructs the slaves to trade with the money; Matthew's slave owner gives no such instruction. There are more differences between the two accounts, but these serve to demonstrate that each writer has a particular intent and relates the parable in such a way as to meet their particular purpose.[2]

This parable illustrates the fact that the use of the Bible in liturgy is not straightforward. Every three years those who gather for worship hear the parable as told by Matthew. These same people never hear (at least not in church) the very different version of the story preserved by Luke. As a community gathered for worship, they are only exposed to the perspective that Matthew brings to the story.

That said, the differences between the two gospel accounts are frequently ironed out. It is not unusual to hear a preacher

95

(consciously or otherwise) blend the two versions. The Gospel set for the day will be that of Matthew, but the sermon will focus on the Lukan re-telling—that of trading the talents. A congregation is urged to use their 'talents' for God. This interpretation has also become popular with fundraising or stewardship campaigns—the text has been domesticated by the institution and used for its own purposes, much as Matthew and Luke used it for theirs. It is possible for a believer to live their whole life without learning—through Matthew—something of the ridiculous generosity of God.

Not only are many congregations left in ignorance about the content of the Bible, but also they are not given the tools (exegetical and hermeneutical) to assist them to make sense of a document, which in many cases is difficult, contradictory and confusing. It is not only the parables that are recorded in different forms; the larger biblical narrative includes distinctive and divergent details. John's gospel is markedly different from the Synoptic gospels to the point that even the preeminent disciples differ. (Peter—so important to the Synoptics—seems to be added as an afterthought by John.) Paul's letters require an understanding of the community to which they were written and the reasons why Paul was writing. Without such information it is impossible to know, for example, why Paul would tell his opponents in Galatia to "castrate themselves" (Gal 5:12).

The primary place in which believers encounter the Bible, which is obviously a complex and difficult text, is in the liturgy.

Liturgy

In addressing the subject of liturgy, we have to recognize that liturgy is primarily a practical expression of faith for worshippers rather than an academic endeavour. Liturgy presupposes faith and is the response of those who believe. It has been defined in a great many ways—from the experiential to the pragmatic. Broadly speaking, it is the pattern of prayer, symbol and text that is used by a people of faith to offer worship to the One in whom they believe, to reinforce and deepen that faith, and to build a community of faith and practice. Liturgy is the event in which the community gathers to engage with the divine. It is a relational activity. Those who believe come to the liturgy in order to be attentive to the divine, and in turn to communicate their hopes and fears to the divine.

The Scriptures are essential to the liturgy. Further, in liturgy the Bible is the text through which the God of faith is made known, and in which the possibility for relationship is described. Faith understands that the Bible has an origin beyond its human creators. Those gathering for worship believe that God continues to speak to them through the Bible as well as through the preacher and the sacraments. In the liturgical context, the Bible is not a passive document, but one that calls for a reaction—both personally and liturgically. As Jesus' parables were intended to move (shock) the hearers from one reality to another, or to open new possibilities, so too "good liturgy disturbs, breaks open, and discloses a new world".[3] The Bible in liturgy is intended to inform, to inspire, to direct, to transform, to encourage, to challenge, and to confront.

For the purpose of this paper, liturgy refers to the activity of Christian believers as they gather to hear the Word and to worship God.

Forming Identity

Liturgy is the occasion on which those who hold a common belief gather together to affirm that belief. In that context, one of the roles of the Bible is that of forming and maintaining the identity of the faith community. The church needs the Bible and the Bible needs the church. The church has no identity outside the book that tells its story, and the book has no life without a community that claims the story as its own. In this sense the Bible is a communal document written by and for particular communities, and continually interpreted by and for those communities of faith.

All of us need to learn who we are and the nature of the community or culture to which we belong. The telling and retelling of the culture's stories is part of this process. As members of the community hear over and over again the stories of that community's origins, its relationships with those around it, of the hurts inflicted or the victories won, so members begin to accept the story as their own. This is no less true for members of the Christian community. As the stories of the Bible are repeated over and over again in liturgy they become for us the story of our own beginnings, our own history. The story that forms the community also unites us and gives us confidence to be who we are in the midst of those who are different. It tells us how to live together and establishes codes of conduct for the community.

In this setting the historical accuracy of the Bible is not relevant. Its stories are the stories of the history of faith, and they recall historical understandings and experiences of God. In liturgy the worshipping community meets the Christ of faith as much as if not more than the Jesus of history. It is only in relatively recent times that there has been a concern with the historicity and reliability of biblical stories. Prior generations accepted them as sacred stories of faith and were not overly concerned with whether or not they corresponded with actual fact.[4]

Worshipers do not come to the liturgy as *tabula rasa* to be formed entirely by the Bible and its stories. Each person brings with them their own story—the hurts and difficulties of their lives, their achievements and their disappointments, their joys and sorrows. The way in which their story interacts with *the* story (the story of faith recorded in the Bible) will affect the ways in which they hear and respond. Those who are marginalized due to gender, poverty or race, as well as those who have been oppressed by colonizing powers or Western civilization, will discover differences within the texts from the educated, white males who have traditionally studied and interpreted the Scriptures for them.

Of course, the story that is used to form a community can also be used to mis-form believers. It can be used to coerce and limit its members, to give to some absolute power and to dis-empower others. The story of a community can be used to imprison rather than to liberate and transform. Religious sects, in particular, have been known to exaggerate selected verses in order to exert control over the group and to ensure compliance even to violence and oppression.

In fact, the history of the Christian faith is testimony to the fact that the Bible has been used to preserve the status quo or to promote and support a particular worldview. Slavery was justified by the use of biblical texts such as Genesis 2, while Colossians 3 has been used to condone domestic violence. The Bible was even used as justification for supporting Hitler's leadership (citing Rom 13:1–7). Despite the fact that 1 Corinthians 11 clearly refers to women praying and prophesying in church, chapter 14 has been used to defend the exclusion of women from ministry. Matt 25:14–30 has been used to justify gross profiteering and exploitation.[5] Schüssler Fiorenza reveals the way in which Luke's account of the sisters Martha and Mary not only censures Martha but also ensures that both women are silenced.[6] Use of biblical texts in such a way has allowed the continued silencing and exclusion of women.

Misinformation leads to mis-formation.

The Lectionary

Mainstream churches have endeavoured to ensure a balanced and comprehensive reading of the Bible in the liturgy in order to prevent its being used in support of narrow and oppressive views. They achieve this goal through the use of a lectionary that determines what is read in the liturgy. In Australia *The Revised Common Lectionary* is used by Anglicans, Lutherans, Roman Catholics and members of the Uniting Church.

Early in the life of the church, and certainly since the fifth century, a system for reading the Bible in the liturgy was developed. At first particular readings were set for feast days, but by the seventh century there had evolved a pattern for reading the Bible in manageable portions and in such a way that the whole Bible could be read over a relatively short period of time. These set readings are gathered together in a lectionary that informs the preacher as to what to read and when.

An advantage of reading the Bible in this way is that it ensures an even coverage of the text. Communities who use a lectionary cannot privilege some parts of the Bible over others or emphasize one aspect of the text over and against another. Neither can they choose to ignore or omit difficult and confronting texts, such as the clear references to genocide and the often-negative attitude towards the Jews. A lectionary means that congregations are forced, for example, to puzzle together over Jesus' praise for the shrewd manager (Luke 16:1) and to worry about the fate of the rich (Matt 6:24; Luke 16:19ff, 18:24–25).

There are disadvantages to this—sometimes arbitrary—division of the Bible into bite-sized pieces. Time constraints mean that the choice of what to read is still selective. Large sections of the Hebrew Bible are omitted, and some of the New Testament is also absent. Sometimes an omission occurs because a similar story/parable occurs elsewhere; sometimes it is because the book or passage contains ideas and language that do not fit with a modern scientific mind. For example, although the language of Revelation is used for congregational responses in the liturgy, the Book of Revelation is read rarely. Some texts are omitted altogether because the ideas expressed in them are not palatable in today's world (for example, Col 3:18ff).

The lectionary makes allowances for modern sensibilities in other ways. When the Psalms are read on a Sunday, those verses that we might find confronting are left out. Thankfully Sunday congregations do not have to read about the heads of babies being dashed against the rocks (Psalm 137). However, this process can lead to a false understanding of the story and of the history of faith. It protects believers from those things that are difficult to come to terms with and creates a situation in which those who believe are poorly equipped to respond to questions about and criticisms of their faith because they have never heard the stories which cause such offense to outsiders.

Further difficulties arise when the Bible is broken into segments suitable for use in liturgy. The first problem relates to the way in which the various books of the Bible are divided. Often this shows little respect for the intentions of the original author/editor. For example, a Sunday reading may begin or end in the middle of a narrative section, breaking the literary integrity. At the same time large sections are sometimes broken into smaller segments that interrupt the flow of the narrative, leaving the preacher to explain what comes before and what follows the text set for the day. Jesus' confrontation with the leaders of the Jews is recorded in chapters 21 and 22 of Matthew's Gospel. However, in order to make the passage manageable for a Sunday time slot, the *Revised Common Lectionary* breaks the chapters into five components, read over five successive weeks. This disturbs the continuity and results in unnecessary repetition of the theme.

In other places the passage chosen by the lectionary may ignore the natural divisions of the text and create breaks with no regard for its meaning or context. For example, Rom 7:14–25—a difficult and complex passage—is made even more difficult to grasp when it is isolated from the context that helps to elucidate its meaning. Read in isolation, the text can be interpreted as

Paul's struggle with sin and sinfulness. However, the exultant cry of Rom 8:1—"There is therefore now no condemnation for those who are in Christ Jesus"—makes it clear that Paul is not weighed down by feelings of guilt and inadequacy. Ideally Rom 7:1–8:17 would be read in one sitting to enable the listener to grasp what Paul is trying to say here.

A second problem is the way in which readings are chosen to fit with the themes and seasons of the church. Mark 1:1–15 is a discrete unit introducing the ministry of Jesus. This passage is not only divided into a number of sub-sections, but those sections are further separated chronologically. The appearance of John the Baptist (Mark 1:1–8) is generally reserved for Advent (November) as it supports the idea of preparation. Jesus' baptism (Mark 1:1–11), which follows on from John's announcement, is reserved for a date in the following January. It is not until the beginning of Lent nearly two months later that Jesus' time in the wilderness and the beginning of Jesus' ministry are read (Mark 1:9–15). The unity of Mark 1:1–15 is seriously disrupted, and it is difficult for any congregation (or preacher) to hear Mark's comparison of John's preaching with that of Jesus.

Readings chosen to be read on feast days often have no regard for the original context or meaning of a passage but are put to use by the writers of the major Western lectionaries to support a tradition that may not be backed by current scholarship. For example, the Gospel reading suggested for the Feast of St John leads us to conclude that the evangelist and the 'Beloved Disciple' are one and the same.

As Elizabeth Smith points out, a "lectionary whose primary function is to proclaim Christ . . . is unlikely to treat the important Jewish Scriptures in other than a simplistic promise-fulfillment manner".[7]

The *Revised Common Lectionary* restricts the choice of readings to passages from the Bible. However, at an earlier point in history, the readings in the liturgy were not limited to those texts that are included in the modern Western Bible. Lives of the saints and other non-canonical texts were included as part of the regular liturgical diet. Worshippers' understanding of their faith was enriched by the knowledge that the faith was derived from a much wider source than that which is preserved in the Hebrew Bible and New Testament. Confining Sunday readings to the canonical texts raises the question as to whether the Bible has exclusive rights to be heard in the liturgy or whether "the exclusion of such a potential treasury" impoverishes worship.[8]

The Sermon

In most liturgies provision is made for a sermon or an exposition of the texts that have been read. This enables a preacher to expound and to interpret the Bible for those present. Many obstacles stand between the text and the listener. These include the translation of the text from the original languages, the process of editing that has brought us the Gospels, the different social context of the original hearers, the way in which the Scripture has been interpreted for the past two thousand years, and the listener's own circumstances. The sermon provides an opportunity to elucidate the meaning of the Bible and to apply it to today's context.

It is the role of the preacher to stand between the community and the text, and to draw out its meaning. Unfortunately there is no guarantee that this will occur. Increased knowledge about the Bible, its writers, and its context has not necessarily been passed on to those who attend the liturgy. The task of interpreting the Bible is sometimes seen as so complex that in practice there is a temptation to over-simplify, to reduce the Bible to simple catch phrases, and to avoid burdening the congregation with anything that is too complex or too challenging. Some clergy take on for themselves the responsibility for deciding what a congregation can and cannot manage, much as Dostoyevsky's Grand Inquisitor took it on himself to protect believers from the freedom that Jesus offered and replaced it with certainty because it was all that he thought they could bear.[9] Further, some clergy seem to "feel a need to protect God by telling little white lies".[10] This tendency both short changes the congregation and leads to misinterpretation or a 'dumbing down' of the text. It also fails to grapple with the truly difficult passages in the Bible—murder, rape, child sacrifice, and so on. Integrity demands that we acknowledge these aspects of our Bible (for if we do not, others will surely use them against us), and that we equip believers to understand and interpret them.

Over forty years ago, James Smart lamented what he described as the "strange silence of the Bible in the Churches".[11] This, he believed, was in part a response to biblical scholarship which he felt had had the effect of making preachers aware of the complexities of interpreting Scripture, and caused them to be unwilling to engage with the discipline and time required to make that scholarship intelligible for their congregations. Some, aware of the difficulties involved, are anxious about applying biblical scholarship to the text in case they get the interpretation wrong. In the short time allotted for preaching, it is easier, he suggests, for the preacher to focus on personal and social issues than to explain the reading for the day. So despite all the advances of biblical scholarship in the twentieth century, believers in the pews are, in general, more ignorant of the central texts of their faith than any generation before them.

This view is supported by Fuller, quoted approvingly by Smith:

> Most worshipers have not been presented with any real alternatives to naïve, pre-critical, devotional use or dogmatic, anti-critical, fundamentalist use. Some parts of the Church have been and still are slow to embrace the potential of historical biblical criticism and the other advances in critical methods that have followed it.[12]

There are grave dangers associated with this failure to grapple with the text. Smart says, "Let the scriptures cease to be heard and soon the remembered Christ becomes the imagined Christ shaped by the religiosity and unconscious desire of his worshippers."[13] Smart places the blame for this situation on the academy—for breaking theological study into different departments and failing to assist the preacher to make the links. Bultmann, on the other hand, points the finger at the failure of scholars to make the connection between their findings and the "life-transforming word of God to man [sic]".[14]

It might more usefully be argued that at least since the Enlightenment, there has been a tendency to 'protect' believers first from scientific discoveries that threatened the 'truth' of the Bible and then from the scientific study of the Bible itself, which revealed contradictions and hidden agendas behind and within the text. As a result, a century (and more) of critical scholarship has not reached the pulpit (and therefore the pews) with the consequence that believers are ill equipped not only to interpret the text for themselves, but also to respond to those like Richard Dawkins who criticize a faith that many educated Christians no longer hold. Many believers are left defending as historical texts documents that have long since been demonstrated to have little basis in history. This complaint about the lack of depth, and in particular the failure to engage in a serious way with the Bible, crosses the whole religious spectrum from Catholic to Evangelical.[15]

At times it seems that the clergy and their congregations are willing to engage in the sort of intellectual schizophrenia that allows them to separate their critical faculties from their emotional responses. Many intelligent, educated believers appear quite willing to leave their intellect at the door of the church. They are content to hear stories and to have their Sunday School faith reinforced rather than challenged and deepened. A former Archbishop of Canterbury, Donald Coggan, warns:

We shall rear a generation of Christians accustomed to the Eucharist but foreigners to many of the great truths of the Christian faith. They have never had the opportunity of listening, Sunday by Sunday, to a steady, intelligent exposition of the things most surely believed among us. They have been fed with snippets, little its and bits, nice thoughts for the day, but nothing, practically nothing, from which bones and spiritual tissue can be built.[16]

In a similar vein, Elizabeth Smith suggests that

over the years Anglican preachers . . . have developed a multitude of ways of avoiding an encounter with the Scripture set for the Sunday service. Sermons have been preached on the collect, . . . on the week's current affairs in parish nation or world . . . on the examination of a saint's life and so on.[17]

Avoiding the Bible takes a number of forms. In some instances, exposition has been replaced by showmanship.[18] Students of homiletics are taught to use illustrations to get the attention of their congregation. All kinds of 'attention getters' are used, from stories, to physical 'props' and, in some cases, even dressing up in costume. Books of sermon illustrations abound. These are usually 'feel-good', devotional stories that purport to be true. The problem is that very often the story itself becomes the text; how wonderful God is, what miracles God performs, how we should care for our neighbours and so on. Meaning is drawn out of the story, but the text of Bible itself is not addressed. There appears to be a belief that intellect and emotion are at different poles and cannot both be engaged at the same time. A common perception that academic sermons are dull fails to acknowledge that topical sermons can be shallow and empty, ignoring the Bible completely.

It has to be said that the best of the mainstream Christian church recognizes the importance of reason, allows for questioning, and exploration, and encourages the application of intellect to faith. For Anglicans and Episcopalians, the current Archbishop of Canterbury puts it this way:

> The strength of the Anglican tradition has been in maintaining a balance between the absolute priority of the Bible, a catholic loyalty to the sacraments and a habit of cultural sensitivity and intellectual flexibility.[19]

In order to be true to ourselves and to respect the texts that we have inherited as the basis of our faith, it is essential to avoid the temptation to trivialize the Bible as it is proclaimed in the liturgy or to patronize congregations by assuming that they do not want (or do not need) to engage fully with the Bible. A preacher should seek to unpack the text and the relevant biblical scholarship in such a way that it can be understood by all those who are present. It is important to face the texts, the situation of the community and the world with integrity and honesty. This can be done by placing the reading in context and by recognizing the ways in which different times, cultures and interest groups have taken the Bible hostage and used it for their own ends.

Critical scholarship need not be treated with suspicion but can be embraced as a tool for enriching the engagement with the text. There a number of ways to reach a deeper understanding of the Bible—for example, by learning that the narrative is structured to build drama and to create a particular effect; or that irony, exaggeration and other rhetorical techniques are employed to make a point, to persuade, to get attention or to increase the likelihood that the story will be remembered. Recognition of these factors will avoid a tendency to literalism and lead to a richer grasp of the faith.

To become well-informed and well-formed Christians, congregations need to hear the gospel as it was intended to be heard. Good preaching that has the courage to declare the gospel allows those who hear to make up their own minds about Jesus, about God and about the Holy Spirit. Preaching that tells the truth can be liberating both intellectually and personally. Many preachers have had the experience of being told by a very relieved member of the congregation that they had always questioned a particular point of view and were so glad to hear that their own deductions had been borne out by scholarship. Believers do not need a university degree to understand that Paul wrote only seven of the letters attributed to him, that the gospel writers wrote with a particular purpose in mind, or that the author of Acts did not intend to write history as we think of history.

Exposition of the Bible provides an opportunity to open other texts that are no longer part of the regular diet. For example, preaching on the parables provides an opportunity to draw on the Gospel of Thomas; a sermon that looks at Martha and Mary allows one to explore the Gospel of Philip.

It is the role of the preacher to expound the text. That this should be done using all the critical tools available would seem to be self-evident. A critical analysis of Scripture goes some way to ensuring that the hearers can form their own opinions not only about the difficult texts, but also about the way in which those texts are used. It is neither possible nor desirable for a preacher (or a biblical scholar for that matter) to keep themselves entirely out of the text. Using critical tools goes some way towards ensuring that the preacher's agenda is limited—and again that those who hear are given the resources to make their own decisions about the text. An approach that is relatively objective avoids the problems of using the Bible to limit and oppress. It opens debate about difficult and controversial texts.

Challenges

Over the centuries the Church has faced changes and challenges—from within and without. In Western Europe, the Reformation led to internal reform and reclaimed the primary place of the Bible in liturgy. The Reformers showed respect for the text. By returning to the original Hebrew and Greek, they tried to discover the original meaning of the text and to escape the allegorical approach that had dominated its interpretation until then. Not only that, but by translating the Bible into the language of the people, they made it accessible to anyone who could read. However, the Enlightenment with its emphasis on scientific proof would later dismiss miracles, the story of creation and many other parts of the Bible as having no scientific or historical basis. At the same time the value of the Bible and its historicity received a blow from which it has never fully recovered.

Today the Christian churches face a number of challenges, not least of which is the decline of numbers in attendance. In both liturgy and preaching this has led to a failure of nerve. We have witnessed a willingness to soften the edges, to repackage both the Bible and the liturgy into forms that might encourage people to attend. In fact, it is possible, as educator Neil Postman has suggested, that we are guilty of "amusing ourselves to death". There is a temptation to embrace reductionism, to satisfy the lowest common denominator.

Conclusion

For many Christians today, the liturgy is the one place in which they regularly encounter the biblical text. It would seem to be self-evident that what they hear through the readings and what they are taught from the pulpit must help them to engage meaningfully with the book that is at the centre of their faith. In a world in which science has refined the methods of research, in which people are no longer content with worn-out answers, it is incumbent on those who read and those who preach to find the Living Word 'behind, in, with and under' the biblical text. This will require an understanding of the various agendas and social settings that led to the Bible as we know it. It will necessitate an examination of the rhetorical and narrative styles used by the various authors to ensure that their message was heard and remembered, and an understanding that the text is now heard and used in new and vastly different contexts. Once the task of deconstruction is completed, it will be possible to proclaim the gospel with a degree of integrity and with confidence.

The situation is critical. Brueggemann suggests that "the misappropriation of Scripture has led to the distortion of life (as of faith) that variously ends in numbness and ache, alienation and rage, restlessness and greed, conformity and autonomy".[20] We must ask ourselves whether in our liturgical life we are guilty of soothing ourselves into a false sense of security by creating a new story, instead of having the courage to examine and try to understand *the* story. A failure to grapple honestly with the biblical texts means that those who hear will have no resources to deal with the difficult issues of injustice and suffering. In considering the Bible and the liturgy we will need to decide whether our task is character development or engagement with the Bible. Is the Bible a guide for living or a living guide? Do we want to search for the meaning of the biblical text, or are we content to read meaning into it? Is it our word or the "Word of the Lord"?

Notes

1. For convenience the names given to the Gospels will be used as shorthand for "the author of" Matthew, etc.

2. The parable as told by Jesus was almost certainly different again, and that version of the parable may well have drawn on preexisting parables in the Jewish tradition. For discussion see: http://www.jesusdatabase.org/index.php?title=178_The_Entrusted_Money.

3. Saliers, quoted by Stephen Burns in lectures to the 2011 Clergy Summer School, in the Diocese of Brisbane.

4. Johnston, *Engaging the Word*, 7.

5. Luz, *Matthew 21–28*, 250.

6. Schüssler Fiorenza, *But She Said*, 53–76.

7. E. J. Smith, *Bearing Fruit in Due Season*, 80.

8. Clark, "Bible and the Liturgy", 26.

9. Dostoyevsky, *The Brothers Karamazov*, 290–305.

10. George Elliot, cited in Smart, *The Strange Silence of the Bible*, 86.

11. Smart, *The Strange Silence of the Bible*.

12. Smith, *Bearing Fruit in Due Season*, 31.

13. Smart, *The Strange Silence of the Bible*, 23.

14. Cited in Smart, *The Strange Silence of the Bible*, 42.

15. Adam, "What Happened to Preaching?", 14–15. See also Smart, *The Strange Silence of the Bible*, 122.

16. Cited in Adam, "Whatever Happened to Preaching?", 15.

17. Smith, *Bearing Fruit in Due Season*, 114.

18. Postman, *Amusing Ourselves to Death*.

19. See his response to a discussion of the Windsor Report by the 75th General Convention of the Episcopal Church (USA), "The Challenge and Hope of Being Anglican Today: A Reflection for the Bishops, Clergy and Faithful of the Anglican Communion": http://www.episcopalchurch.org/3577_76411_ENG_HTM.html.

20. Brueggeman, *Finally, Comes the Poet*, 47–48.

7

Scripture, Science and the Big Story

Peter Catt

The human world of today has not grown cold but is ardently searching for a God proportionate to the new dimensions of a Universe whose appearance has completely revolutionized the scale of our faculty of worship.[1]

Once upon a time . . .

Storytelling is one of the characteristics that make us human. Jack Niles[2] contends that storytelling is so foundational to human nature that our scientific name should be changed to *Homo narrans* (storytelling human). The weaving of stories appears to be a uniquely human activity. Other creatures are intelligent, make tools, cultivate the earth and concoct plans to increase the chances of a successful hunt, but only we humans tell stories.

The Role of Story

Film, TV drama, history and novels are just some of the ways in which humans tell stories. Stories make up what we call 'The News' and are the way we capture our family histories. All history is story. Even science, which often sees itself as engaged in an activity that is more sophisticated than storytelling, communicates its findings through various forms of narrative.

We create stories because we are conscious, intelligent, and seem to be hardwired to want to make sense of life through the discovery of meaning. Our greatest fear is meaninglessness or lack of purpose. We know all too well the effect that not having a positive life-story has on the unemployed and on others who feel forgotten by society. We want to know that life has a purpose. "Everything happens for a reason," we say.

The former Archbishop of Canterbury, Rowan Williams,[3] notes that we humans need systems of meaning because they allow us to see phenomena in connected rather than arbitrary ways. Connection gives a sense of order. Arbitrariness is associated with chaos.

Through stories we confront and deal with what has been called 'The Existential Question'. This can be formed in various ways: Why are we here? What is the purpose of life? What am I here for? The Monty Python team in their movie *The Meaning of Life*, particularly in the theme song, captured this question delightfully:

> Is life just a game where we make up the rules
> While we're searching for something to say,
> Or are we just simply spiraling coils
> Of self-replicating DNA?[4]

Metanarrative

A metanarrative is a particular type of story, one that makes sense of life and conveys meaning at a 'global level'. It is an all-encompassing story that provides a complete explanation for the way life is lived and makes sense of a society's history.[5] In short, it captures and expresses our 'worldview'. It is a story about a story, providing a meaning-making context for the many 'little stories' that make up life.

As part of their critique of 'metanarrative', postmodern philosophers, beginning with Jean-François Lyotard, suggest that a metanarrative is often an untold story that unifies and 'totalizes' the world. They suggest that this 'totalizing' aspect prevents people from looking at life through other lenses and so legitimizes and normalizes harmful power structures.[6] As an aside, it is worth noting that even those who criticize the way metanarratives work on and through us tend to weave a metanarrative of their own as they do so.[7] We cannot help but frame our life within a story context.

Because metanarratives are global, they take us beyond our individual story, often demonstrating how our sense of purpose can be derived from our origins. They allow us to see that our sense of who we are comes from our connection to our beginning. They express our purpose for being. Hence metanarratives are humanity's ultimate tool for banishing the fear of meaninglessness and providing 'the' answer to the existential question, referred to above.

The Christendom Metanarrative

For the best part of two thousand years, Western society was undergirded by the 'Christendom' metanarrative. This expressed a worldview that was based on a western interpretation of the biblical writings. This worldview gave the frame that shaped and supported the stories and practices of Western culture following the adoption of Christianity as the state religion of the Roman Empire during the reign of Constantine. The Christendom metanarrative deals with our origins, with the purpose of creation and also gives meaning to human existence. It is also a story about the ultimate fate of the earth and its people. This metanarrative contains a number of assumptions:

1. There is a God who is the creative principle.
2. God is not capricious but driven by justice, mercy, and love.
3. The universe is ordered.
4. The universe has a purpose.
5. History is charged with the presence of the Divine.
6. God has an active interest in the outflowing of human life. Human life matters because it matters to God.

Those who inhabit this worldview seek to understand humanity and history against the backdrop created by the above-mentioned assumptions. Many of our 'little stories' therefore record the wrestling of the generations as they seek to determine how they fit into the world that God has created and ordered.

The worldview expressed in the Christendom metanarrative provided the frame that allowed for a specific and spectacular place to be given to the story of the life, death, and resurrection of Jesus. Looked at through the particular set of lenses of the Christendom metanarrative, the Jesus story is seen to be of cosmological significance. It allows for suffering to be viewed in a new and meaningful way. One is also given the opportunity to look at the world through the eyes of the vulnerable and marginalized. The Jesus story is understood to indicate that God cares about humanity, and that life has an eternal and ultimate purpose. This purpose can be reflected in life as lived in the present; overturning the notion that life might be meaningless or that it might best be expressed through a 'dog-eat-dog' way of being. In other words, the birth, death, and resurrection of Jesus place human life and destiny within an eschatological context.

As noted above, the Christendom metanarrative is undergirded by the assumption that there is a God who has produced a universe that is ordered. Over time this led to a reduction in the power of superstition, and in the fullness of time paved the way for the birth of science in the West. This story provided the assumptions on which scientific method is built; assumptions that still cannot be tested or proven.

Modern Western culture, then, is the product of the Christendom metanarrative. This in turn gave birth to the Enlightenment metanarrative; a worldview that began to emerge in the seventeenth century. This promoted the supremacy of reason, affirmed the human as separate from the rest of creation, which came to be labelled as nature, and paved the way for humans to dominate rather than coexist. Increasingly the 'tellers' of this story have seen it as displacing the Christendom metanarrative and therefore the need for God. The 'new atheists' are an expression of this metanarrative.

The Dangers of a Common Story

As mentioned previously, postmodern philosophers have described the capacity for metanarratives to prevent people from recognizing the power structures that affect their lives. This was very important work that demonstrated how the Christendom metanarrative could be used by the powerful to justify and maintain their power. Such use is summed up in the original words of the nineteenth-century hymn, *All Things Bright and Beautiful* by Cecil F. Alexander:

> The rich man in his castle,
> The poor man at his gate,
> God made them, high or lowly,
> And ordered their estate.

Feminist and liberationist theologians have demonstrated how the Christendom story has been used as an oppressive weapon. Biblical criticism has aided this by demythologizing the biblical stories, identifying different literary genre, and distancing faith-based documents from 'history', as those influenced by the Enlightenment have come to understand it.

Lyotard and those he inspired suggested that we could do away with the totalitarianism of grand narratives by developing a number of stories that are less grand in scale. These 'little stories' could compete with each other and be alive together in a community at one and the same time.[8]

The postmodern critique and the breakdown of the power of metanarrative for other reasons, which will be explored in the next section, have seen people in the West tending toward the practice of generating meaning for themselves by creating and telling their 'own story'. One downside to this is that it can give birth to relativism: my approach to life is just as valid as yours. In other words it can lead to the belief that there are no universal values. This reduced scope for storytelling also begs the question of what is the place of community in our 'personal' stories. Are the world we live in and the community we share life with just the backdrop against which we tell our personal stories, or are they something more? Is not our community a living entity that has a story of its own? A world made up exclusively of personal stories is not capable of dealing with our relationship, at a corporate level, to other creatures, and to the planet as whole.

The Loss of a Common Story

A few years ago I was sitting with an elder of an aboriginal community. We were discussing the importance of story to human flourishing. The elder suggested that perhaps the time had come for the people of that place to recapture their aboriginality by 'making up' some Dreaming stories. The Dreamtime is the metanarrative base for the many Australian aboriginal nations. It captures and governs their understanding of their relationship to the land and the expression of culture, and is the bedrock upon which their society is built. Most of the original Dreamtime stories belonging to the nation in question had been lost as the story custodians died. The elder recognized that the inherent racism of the non-indigenous community in which they found themselves continued to deny a place for Aborigines in the mainstream 'story'. As a result they were a people without a story and therefore a people without a sense of identity or a sense of purpose. It seemed to this elder that the way forward was to recreate a story world that made sense for them and which would give them a sense of dignity, purpose, and life.

That elder's story reminds us that many indigenous peoples throughout the world have found themselves without a life-giving meta-story to live under. The metanarrative that undergirded their traditional culture is often lost to them and access to the 'new world' is denied by racism or economic disadvantage. When a people lose their story, they literally become lost to themselves.

John Carroll[9] suggests that the postmodern deconstruction of metanarratives and the scientific focus on reason has led to the Western world losing its sense of direction and purpose; that 'it is dying for the want of a good story'. Edward Edinger captures the effects of this well:

> The breakdown of a central myth is like the shattering of a vessel containing a precious essence; the fluid is spilled and drains away, soaked up by the surrounding undifferentiated matter. Meaning is lost. In its place, primitive and atavistic contents are reactivated. Differentiated values disappear and are replaced by the elemental motivations of power and pleasure, or else the individual is exposed to emptiness and despair.[10]

The West finds itself in this difficult place, in part, because of the 'falling out' between the Christendom story and its child, the Enlightenment metanarrative. Critical biblical scholarship, which is a child of the Enlightenment, has also contributed to this situation.

The clash between these two worldviews stems, in large measure, from a lack of explicit understanding of how narrative works for us. Movements such as narratology, and narrative theology, which I see as helping to provide a way forward, and which will be introduced shortly, were still some way off when the two stories began to clash, and so the lack of understanding of the role of story had us fighting the wrong battles.

The Enlightenment's focus on reason, and therefore facts, and the story it told about humans as a result, led to a discounting of other ways of knowing and truth telling. As a result stories that were not 'history' were dismissed as childish, and faith stories became little more than superstition. Factual stories became the only valid form of narrative. The 'new atheists' reflect this understanding.

The problem was compounded by the ways in which those who inhabited a 'faith story world' sought to defend their position. These mostly tried to deal with the Enlightenment on its own turf. This saw some accepting the Enlightenment worldview to the point where they debunked their own metanarrative, while others developed the 'god-of-the-gaps' concept. This idea accepts explanations offered by science while at the same time suggesting that God is responsible for the 'mysterious' aspects of life; those which science cannot explain. A third group sought to use quasi-scientific methods to prove that the myths of the Bible were history and that the faith-based worldview was, in fact, scientific. The first approach saw God eliminated from the scene; the second had God retreating to the ever-receding edges of the universe; while the third saw 'facts' being defended against the evidence. Modern-day deists and creationists encapsulate these understandings. The result was that each of these approaches affirmed and strengthened the Enlightenment worldview and its understanding of truth and truth telling. In so doing, they colluded in the destruction of a meaning-rich metanarrative.

Such approaches were always doomed to fail because they did not appreciate the role of story in human life; the narrative metanarrative, if you like. The net result is that we are now scrambling for meaning at the 'meta' level, as witnessed by the increasing sense of hopelessness and fear one sees within religious groups and in the wider community.[11]

Moving Towards
a New 'Meta' Story

Whilst an understandable development in the history of human storytelling, the postmodern response to the power of metanarrative, which has seen individuals developing their own meaning, does not provide a rich enough soil to allow for human flourishing. The work of sociologist Peter Berger gives us some clues as to why this is so. Berger, while suspicious of religion, also suggests that social reality is a form of consciousness. This means that an individual's conception of reality is produced by his or her interaction with social structures.[12] In other words, for an individual's story to make sense and convey meaning, it needs to be part of the larger 'Story'. We need a metanarrative if we are to make sense of life. We know deep down that our lives are more than just our own story. We are the product of our relationships.

This need is further evidenced by the fact that movements that have dismissed the Christendom metanarrative in particular, and the role of metanarrative in general, are operating in ways that demonstrate that they also are operating under the influence of metanarratives. As noted previously, the postmodern critique is an embodiment of a metanarrative which casts humans as individuals who can craft meaning for themselves. And the 'new atheism' is based on the Enlightenment understanding of the human. One of the key assumptions found in both of these 'stories' is captured by Descartes' pithy statement, "I think therefore I am." It is assumed that we are rational and reasonable creatures, and that meaning is to be found simply through the act of thinking and through the satisfaction of curiosity.

These are impoverished metanarratives. They cast us as separate and separated. The second, which sees truth as facts only, presents a humanity impoverished by the absence of truth-telling as revealed and captured in poetry, art and music. Also inadequate is the push for the recapturing of the religion of our fore-*fathers* [*sic*] that sees religious fundamentalists worldwide clinging to a now-dead story that leads them to contend that the findings of science are not true.

All this points us to the need for a more sophisticated metanarrative that entertains the deepest of human yearnings and honours our complexity, as emotional and spiritual beings as well as rational creatures.

Narrative Theology

Narrative theology was developed in response to critical biblical scholarship during the latter half of the last century. Key players in its development were George Lindbeck and Hans Wilhelm Frei.

Narrative theology suggests that the Bible should be seen as containing a collection of narratives rather than a set of coherent theological propositions. In other words it accepts the findings of biblical criticism that there is not one single and coherent theology within the Bible, but rather a set of theologies. Narrative theology contends that meaning is to be found by reflecting on the stories found in Scripture. The catechumenal movement within the various churches has embraced this way of using the Bible, encouraging community members to find their place in the meta-story found in the Scriptures by engaging with the individual narratives the biblical writers have recorded. By reflecting on the way the individual narratives touch their lives and by seeking to uncover the invitations that lead to a transformed way of living and to ministry, individuals find themselves being formed and shaped by the meta-story.

All stories are written within a context, and the use of narrative theology allows a responsive and synergistic response that takes into account the way we see 'life, the universe, and everything' now. It allows faith communities to reflect on the meta-story they have inherited, find its grand themes and then re-express them within and for a new context.

Such an approach acknowledges, for example, that the creation stories found in Genesis 1 and 2 were written in and for a time when people understood the universe to be a three-tiered structure: God in heaven, earth in the middle, and the underworld below. It accepts that the writers expressed, and searched for, meaning against that backdrop. It also sees that over time our understandings of the age of the universe and its structure have evolved, and that as a result the backdrop against which the human story is cast, and needs to be understood, has also changed. We no longer understand that God is in the clouds. The heaven described in the Bible has become a difficult construct. But the quest for meaning remains, the deep longings of the human heart are just as profoundly felt, and the grand themes of the Christendom metanarrative and other faith worldviews still express something of the dignity of humanity. People have a need to know that they matter; not only to others, but to time and eternity; that they matter to God. They still need to honour the sense of presence and purpose they experience, and to be given the tools to live in a world charged with that presence. To be fully and truly human we need to be able to quest after, and find, meaning. We need to express our deep longings and to honour the grand 'meta' themes in a context that takes seriously the world as we now know it to be. In saying this we need also to note that over time our understanding of the physical world will shift again and that we will need to recast the detail of the story again and again.

Testing Stories

As new metanarratives develop—for develop them we have and will—we shall do well to take to heart the lessons we have learnt from the experience of losing our common story, from the critique of metanarratives, from the gifts of biblical criticism, and from the clashes that led to the collapse of the Christendom metanarrative. All these are now part of our human story. We cannot put the 'genie back in the bottle', nor should we desire to do so. Our story contains failures from which we need to learn, and 'the getting of wisdom' can be part of our narrative. We have learnt that we are hardwired storytellers, and that stories can be destructive when misused by the powerful. Stories possess the power 'to make' and 'to break' us. This 'little story' about the power of story is now part of our meta-story, the narrative's metanarrative, and we do well to take this awareness with us. As noted in the previous section, 'metanarratives' develop spontaneously, for that is what we do, and so we do well to take what we have learnt into our use of any new story.

We now have the capacity to recognize our need for a meta-story. The 'scales have fallen from our eyes', and as a result we have the ability to assess that which was once unrecognized bedrock. We can make choices and give permission for a story to be ours. We have freedom to own or reject stories; a privilege that has not been afforded to previous generations. We are now able to name the assumptions that lie under our understanding of ourselves and our world. With this new freedom comes the responsibility to test stories before we sign up to them. We can make choices about which assumptions we are going to allow to shape us and our comprehension of the world. Having stated this, one also needs to acknowledge that these statements are themselves based on assumptions about human capacity and so reflect a particular metanarrative. Such awareness has the potential to be the lasting gift of both postmodern critique and critical biblical scholarship.

The Context for a
Twenty-First-Century Western Metanarrative

All stories—both 'meta' and small—arise within their context, and so reflect, capture, and become beholden to a particular understanding of the world. A number of developments have affected our worldview over the last few centuries and these need to be noted as we seek to uncover and express a new metanarrative; the story that will carry the sense of human purpose and meaning for our time.

In my view the most profound influence on our worldview in recent times has been science. The scientific worldview and scientific method have taught us to look for cause and effect, to be open to the new, and to be sceptical. Various branches of science have shown us previously unknown things about the nature of the universe, including its size and organization. Astronomy, for example, not only overturned the assumption that the sun went around the earth but also pointed us towards an appreciation of the magnitude of space-time. As a result our sense of the presence of the Divine began to retreat and 'a heaven beyond the Universe' became a very remote thing indeed. Many took refuge in a spiritualized notion of heaven, but that too is distant from the world. A spiritualized god is of no earthly use. Further, biology and cosmology have shown us that we have 'become' gradually rather than being plonked, fully and finally formed, on the earth during a seven-day creative process. We live in an evolving universe.

Another profound change in human self-understanding has come through the discoveries of quantum physics. Quantum physics' insights into the universe are so radical that they challenge not only many of the assumptions that drove the Christendom metanarrative but also the assumptions lying behind the Enlightenment metanarrative. Quantum physics invites us to sit lightly with concepts such as 'objective', 'observer', and 'individual'. It invites us to see ourselves as being integrated in and integral to a complex relational system; that we are, in fact, the product of our relationships.

Quantum physics' questioning of the assumptions undergirding the Enlightenment metanarrative has provided an opening for the expression of disquiet as to where the Enlightenment metanarrative might have been leading us. Scientific reductionism, the selfish gene, and the idea that love could be reduced to an expression of the reproductive urge, do not speak to who we are or to how we see ourselves, reducing us as they do to biological processes in a utilitarian way. The fact that music moves us and we still want to speak of the experience we call love suggests that a metanarrative built entirely on reason and 'fact' does not capture who we see ourselves to be and, more importantly, what we aspire to be. Being fully human is an aspirational pastime.

One Possible New Story

Applying the insights of science, critical biblical scholarship, and narrative theology to our context might work something like this. The grand themes in the Bible invite us to appreciate that the universe exists for a purpose and that the created order is moving towards some form of fulfilment. They also hold that the Divine is involved, interested, and personal; longing for humanity to find its true self through the pursuit of love and justice; and that human purpose and meaning are most clearly expressed in the life of Jesus of Nazareth. Science has revealed that the universe is immense, ancient, evolving, and relational. The physical nature of the universe and the mode of its becoming suggest that we live a world in which our destiny is inextricably linked to the fate of the universe. Taken together, these invite us to appreciate that the story we tell about ourselves needs to be a 'very big one.' It needs to be cosmological and eschatological.

The work of the priest-scientist, Pierre Teilhard de Chardin, shows one way that all this can be brought together. Teilhard was convinced that evolution was a key to understanding the universe. When he combined this scientific insight with the grand narratives of the Bible, he concluded that evolution was not a random process but one that was being drawn by the Divine to the 'Omega point'.[13] He saw that evolution had a purpose, and that humans as conscious agents in the universe could be active agents in the becoming of the cosmos. Further, he argued that the Incarnation of Christ had led to a twinning of the evolution of the cosmos (*cosmogenesis*) with the evolution of Christ (*Christogenesis*). He thus invites us to embrace an evolutionary metanarrative with eschatological import.

John F. Haught expresses it like this:

Just rearrange the religious furniture in your mind a little. Think of the world not so much as leaning on the past, and don't think of creation as something that takes place exclusively in the past, but think of the world as always "resting on the future", a future that for Teilhard is ultimately nothing other than God. God is the world's future, and it is as future that God is the world's ultimate support. In this reconfiguration it is not inconceivable that the vine of religious meaning that traditionally wound itself around the vertical hierarchical latticework can now be transformatively rewound around the horizontal-evolutionary picture of a still unfinished creation.[14]

In this worldview humans are co-creators of the future. Such a metanarrative allows religion and science to be seen as partners in human self-understanding. Here religion does not cut across or compete with science but honours it while adding the layers of hope, meaning, and purpose that we need to be fully human. Ewert Cousins captures these sentiments in the form of a hymn:

Creative energy of the cosmos,
Love that unites atoms and humans,
That through convergence
Creates new possibilities,
Fill human consciousness
With divine grace.
Creative love energy,
Infuse the divine milieu
With energizing love
And bring all creation
To the completion of Omega.[15]

Notes

1. de Chardin, *The Future of Man*, 268.
2. Niles, *Homo Narrans*, 3.
3. Williams, *Dostoevsky*, vii.

4. Lyrics by Trevor Jones and Eric Idle.

5. Stephens, *Retelling Stories*, 3.

6. Lyotard, *The Postmodern Condition*, xxiv.

7. Callinicos, *Against Postmodernism*, 3–5.

8. Lyotard, *Postmodern Condition*, 60–66.

9. Carroll, *Western Dreaming*, 6–12.

10. Edinger, *The Creation of Consciousness*, 9–10.

11. Marr, *Panic*.

12. Berger, *The Social Construction of Reality*, 150–55.

13. de Chardin, *Phenomenon of Man*, 288.

14. Cited in Salmon and Farina, *The Legacy of Pierre Teilhard de Chardin*, 22–23.

15. Salmon and Farina, *The Legacy of Pierre Teilhard de Chardin*, 58.

Works Consulted

A Prayer Book for Australia. Melbourne: Broughton Publishing, 1995.

Adam, David. "Whatever Happened to Preaching?" Pp. 14–28 in Keith Weller, *'Please! No More Boring Sermons': Preaching for Australians; Contemporary Insights and Practical Aspects*. Melbourne: Acorn Press, 2007.

Allchin, Arthur Macdonald. "Anglican Spirituality". Pp. 351–64 in *The Study of Anglicanism*. Ed. Stephen Sykes, John Booty, and Jonathan Knight. London: SPCK, 2004.

Alston, William P. "The Autonomy of Religious Experience". *International Journal of Religious Experience* 31 (1992): 68–87.

Armstrong, J. *Looking at Pictures: An Introduction to the Appreciation of Art*. London: Duckworth, 1996.

Armstrong, Karen. *The Battle for God*. New York, NY: Knopf, 2009.

———. *The Bible: A Biography*. New York, NY: Atlantic Monthly Press, 2007.

Armstrong, Regis J., and Ignatius C. Brady. *Francis and Clare: The Complete Works*. New York, NY: Paulist Press, 1982.

Avis, Paul. *The Identity of Anglicanism: Essentials of Anglican Ecclesiology*. New York, NY: T & T Clark, 2010.

Barr, James. *Holy Scripture: Canon, Authority, Criticism*. Oxford: Clarendon, 1983.

———. *The Bible in the Modern World*. London: SCM Press, 1973.

Bartlett, Alan. *A Passionate Balance: The Anglican Tradition*. New York, NY: Orbis, 2007.

Beal, Timothy K. *The Rise and Fall of the Bible: The Unexpected History of an Accidental Book*. Chicago, IL: Houghton Mifflin Harcourt, 2011.

Berger, Peter L. and Luckmann, Thomas. *The Social Construction of Reality: A Treatise in the Sociology of Knowledge*. Garden City, NY: Anchor, 1967.

Billings, Alan. *Making God Possible: The Task of Ordained Ministry Present and Future*. London: SPCK, 2010.

Borg, Marcus J. *Reading the Bible Again for the First Time: Taking the Bible Seriously but Not Literally.* San Francisco, CA: HarperSanFrancisco, 2001.

Borg, Marcus J. and N. T. Wright. *The Meaning of Jesus: Two Visions.* San Francisco, CA: HarperSanFrancisco, 1999.

Briggs, Richard S. *Reading the Bible Wisely: An Introduction to Taking Scripture Seriously.* Rev. ed. Eugene, OR: Cascade Books, 2011.

———. "Scripture in Christian Formation: Pedagogy, Reading Practice and Scriptural Exemplars". *Theology* 114,2 (2011): 83–90.

Brown, Jeannine, K., Carla, M. Dhal, and Wyndy Corbin Reuschling. *Becoming Whole and Holy: An Integrative Conversation about Christian Formation.* Grand Rapids, MI: Baker Academic, 2011.

Brueggemann, Walter. *The Word That Redescribes the World: The Bible and Discipleship.* Minneapolis, MN: Fortress Press, 2011.

———. *An Introduction to the Old Testament: The Canon and Christian Imagination.* Louisville, KY: Westminster John Knox Press, 2003.

———. *Finally, Comes the Poet: Daring Speech for Proclamation.* Minneapolis, MN: Fortress Press, 1989.

Bultmann, Rudolf. *History of the Synoptic Tradition.* San Francisco, CA: Harper San Francisco, 1976.

Burke, P. "Overture: The New History, Its Past and Its Future". Pp. 1–23 in *New Perspectives in Historical Writing.* Ed. P. Burke. Cambridge, UK: Polity Press, 1991.

Burns, Stephen. "Worship, Formation and Small Seminary Communities". *Australian Journal of Liturgy* 12,3 (2011): 142–48.

Butler, Christopher. *Postmodernism: A Very Short Introduction.* Oxford: Oxford University Press, 2002.

Cadwallader, Alan H., ed. *Hermeneutics and the Authority of Scripture.* Adelaide: ATF Theology, 2011.

Callinicos, Alex. *Against Postmodernism: A Marxist Critique.* Cambridge, UK: Polity Press, 1991.

Campbell, Antony F. *Making Sense of the Bible: Difficult Texts and Modern Faith.* Mahwah, NJ: Paulist Press, 2010.

Carnley, Peter. *Reflections in Glass: Trends and Tensions in the Contemporary Anglican Church.* Sydney: HarperCollins, 2004.

Carr, Edward Hallett. *What is History?* Rev. ed. Hampshire, UK: Palgrave, 2001.

Carroll, John. *Western Dreaming: The Western World Is Dying for Want of a Story.* Sydney: HarperCollins Publishers, 2001.

Chapman, Raymond. *Means of Grace, Hope of Glory: Five Hundred Years of Anglican Thought.* Norwich, UK: Canterbury Press, 2005.

Clark, Neville. "The Bible and the Liturgy". Pp. 23–29 in *Getting the Liturgy Right: Essays by the Joint Liturgical Group on Practical Liturgical Principles for Today.* Ed. Ronald C. D. Jasper. London: SPCK, 1982

Coleman, Simon, and Peter Collins. *Religion, Identity and Change: Perspectives on Global Transformations.* Surrey, UK: Ashgate, 2004.

Conner, Steven. *Postmodern Culture: An Introduction to Theories of the Contemporary.* Oxford: Blackwell, 1989.

Countryman, L. William. *The Poetic Imagination: An Anglican Spiritual Tradition.* New York, NY: Orbis Press, 1999.

———. *Biblical Authority or Biblical Tyranny? Scripture and the Christian Pilgrimage.* Harrisburg, PA: Trinity Press International, 1994.

Cowdell, Scott, and Muriel Porter, eds. *Lost in Translation? Anglicans, Controversy and the Bible: Perspectives from the Doctrine Commission of the Anglican Church of Australia.* Thornbury, Australia: Desbooks, 2004.

Crossan, John Dominic. *The Historical Jesus: The Life of a Mediterranean Jewish Peasant.* San Francisco, CA: Harper Collins, 1991.

Davis, Ellen F. "Reading the Bible Confessionally in the Church." *Anglican Theological Review* 84,1 (2002): 25–35.

Dawkins, Richard. *The God Delusion.* Boston, MA: Houghton Mifflin, 2006.

De Saussure, Ferdinand. *Writings in General Linguistics*. Oxford: Oxford University Press, 2006.

Derrida, Jacques. *Of Grammatology*. Baltimore, MD: John Hopkins University Press, 1976.

Dostoyevsky, Fyodor Mikhailovich. *The Brothers Karamazov*. Trans. David Magarshack. Middlesex, UK: Penguin Books, 1958

Edinger, Edward F. *Creation of Consciousness: Jung's Myth for Modern Man*. Studies in Jungian Psychology. Toronto: Inner City Books, 1984.

Ehrman, Bart D. *Lost Christianities: The Battles for Scripture and the Faiths We Never Knew*. Oxford: Oxford University Press, 2005.

———. *Misquoting Jesus: The Story Behind Who Changed the Bible and Why*. San Francisco, CA: Harper, 2005.

Everitt, Nicholas and Alec Fisher. *Modern Epistemology: A New Introduction*. London: McGraw-Hill, 1995.

Fitzgerald, John, Fika J. van Rensburg and Herrie van Rooy, eds. *Animosity, the Bible, and Us: Some European, North American, and South African Perspectives*, Society of Biblical Literature Global Perspectives on Biblical Scholarship 12. Atlanta, GA: Society of Biblical Literature, 2009.

Fitzmyer, Joseph A. "Catholic Principles for Interpreting Scripture: A Study of the Pontifical Biblical Commission's the Interpretation of the Bible in the Church". *Biblica* 83,3 (2002): 434–39.

Flanagan, Kieran. Preface. Pp. viii–xii in *Religion, Identity and Change: Perspectives on Global Transformations*. Ed. Simon Coleman and Peter Collins. Aldershot, UK: Ashgate, 2004.

Flesseman-van Leer, Ellen, ed. *The Bible: Its Authority and Interpretation in the Ecumenical Movement*, Faith and Order Paper, 99. Geneva: World Council of Churches, 1980.

Fee, Gordon D. *Paul's Letter to the Philippians*. New International Commentary on the New Testament. Grand Rapids, MI: Eerdmans, 1995.

Foster, Charles R., Lisa Dahill, Larry Golemon, and Barbara Wang Tolentino. *Educating Clergy: Teaching Practices and Pastoral Imagination*. Stanford, CA: Jossey-Bass, 2006.

Fredriksen, Paula. "What Does Jesus Have to Do with Christ?" Pp. 3–17 in *Christology: Memory, Inquiry, Practice*. Ed. A. M. Clifford and A. J. Godzieba. New York, NY: Orbis Books, 2003.

Goldingay, John. *Models for Interpretation of Scripture*. Ontario: Clements Publishing Co., 2004.

———. *Models for Scripture*. Grand Rapids, MI: Eerdmans, 1994.

———. "Inspiration and Inerrancy". Pp. 261–81 in *Models for Scripture*. Grand Rapids, MI: Eerdmans, 1994.

Goulder, Michael and John Hick. *Why Believe in God?* London: SCM Press, 1983.

Haack, Susan. "A Foundherentist Theory of Empirical Justification". Pp. 237–47 in *The Theory of Knowledge: Classical and Contemporary Readings*. Ed. L. P. Pojman. Belmont, CA: Wadsworth, 2003.

———. *Evidence and Inquiry: Towards Reconstruction in Epistemology*. Oxford: Blackwell Publishers, 1993, 1995.

Hedrick, Charles W., ed. *When Faith Meets Reason: Religion Scholars Reflect on Their Spiritual Journeys*. Santa Rosa, CA: Polebridge, 2008.

Heyward, Carter. "Breaking Point". Pp. 9–33 in *Through Us, With Us, In Us: Relational Theologies in the Twenty First Century*. Ed. Lisa Isherwood and Elaine Bellchambers. London: SCM Press, 2010.

Hitchens, Christopher. *God is Not Great: How Religion Poisons Everything*. New York, NY: Twelve, 2007.

Hooks, Bell. *Teaching Critical Thinking: Practical Wisdom*. New York, NY: Routledge, 2010.

———. *Teaching Community: A Pedagogy of Hope*. New York, NY: Routledge, 2003.

Hoover, Roy W., ed. *Profiles of Jesus*. Santa Rosa, CA: Polebridge Press, 2002.

Irvine, C., ed. *Anglican Liturgical Identity: Papers from the Prague Meeting of the International Anglican Liturgical Consultation*. Norwich, UK: Canterbury Press, 2008.

Jenks, Gregory C. *The Once and Future Bible: An Introduction to the Bible for Religious Progressives*. Eugene, OR: Wipf & Stock, 2011.

Johnson, Luke Timothy. *The Real Jesus: The Misguided Quest for the Historical Jesus and the Truth of the Traditional Gospels.* San Francisco, CA: Harper Collins, 1996.

Johnstone, Michael. *Engaging the Word.* The New Church's Teaching Series 3. Boston, MA: Cowley Publications, 1998.

Kane, Robert. "The Ends of Metaphysics". *International Philosophical Quarterly* 33 (1993): 431–28.

Keating, James F. "Epistemology and the Theological Application of Jesus Research". Pp. 18–43 in *Christology: Memory, Inquiry, Practice.* Ed. A. M. Clifford and A. J. Godzieba. New York, NY: Orbis Books, 2003.

Kittredge, Cynthia Briggs, Ellen Bradhsaw Aitken, and Jonathan A. Draper, eds. *The Bible in the Public Square: Reading the Signs of the Times.* Minneapolis, MN: Fortress, 2008.

Kugler, Robert, and Patrick Hartin. *An Introduction to the Bible.* Grand Rapids, MI: Eerdmans, 2009.

Larson-Miller, Lizette. "Seminary Chapel in a Prayer Book Context". Pp. 81–99 in *Common Worship in Theological College.* Ed. Siobhan Garrigan and Todd E. Johnson. Salem, OR: Wipf & Stock, 2010.

Leaves, Nigel. *Religion Under Attack: Getting Theology Right!* Salem, OR: Polebridge Press, 2011.

Lonergan, Bernard. *Love and Objectivity in Virtue Ethics.* Toronto: University of Toronto Press, 2008

Lyotard, Jean-Francois. *The Postmodern Condition: A Report on Knowledge.* Theory and History of Literature, 10. Minneapolis, MN: University of Minnesota Press, 1984.

Luz, Ulrich. *Matthew 21–28: A Commentary.* Hermeneia. Minneapolis, MN: Fortress Press, 2005.

McEvoy, James. "Narrative or History?—A False Dilemma: The Theological Significance of the Historical Jesus". *Pacifica* 14 (2001): 279–80.

McGrath, Alister E. *Christian Theology: An Introduction.* 4th ed. Oxford: Blackwell, 2007.

McIntyre, John. *The Shape of Christology: Studies in the Doctrine of the Person of Christ.* 2nd ed. Edinburgh: T & T Clark, 1998.

Mack, Burton L. *Who Wrote the New Testament?: The Making of the Christian Myth*. San Francisco, CA: Harper Collins, 1995.

Marr, David. *Panic*. Collingwood, Australia: Black Inc. Publishers, 2011.

Marshall, William. *Scripture, Tradition and Reason: A Selective View of Anglican Theology Through the Centuries*. Dublin: The Columba Press, 2010.

Martin, Dale B. *Pedagogy on the Bible: An Analysis and Proposal*. London: Westminster John Knox Press, 2008.

Migliore, Daniel L. *Faith Seeking Understanding: An Introduction to Christian Theology*. 2nd ed. Grand Rapids, MI: Eerdmans, 2004.

Miller, Robert J., ed. *The Future of the Christian Tradition*. Santa Rosa, CA: Polebridge, 2007.

———., ed. *The Apocalyptic Jesus: A Debate*. Santa Rosa, CA: Polebridge Press, 2001.

The New Shorter Oxford English Dictionary. New York, NY: Oxford University Press, 1993.

Nietzsche, Friedrich. *Thus Spoke Zarathustra: A Book for None and All*. Trans. Walter Kaufman. New York, NY: Random House; reprinted in *The Portable Nietzsche*. New York, NY: The Viking Press, 1954 and Harmondsworth, UK: Penguin Books, 1976.

Niles, John D. *Homo Narrans: The Poetics and Anthropology of Oral Literature*. Philadelphia, PA: University of Pennsylvania Press, 1999.

Oakeshott, Michael. "The Activity of Being an Historian". Pp. 69–95 in *The History of Ideas: An Introduction to Method*. Ed. Preston King. London: Croom Helm, 1983).

Ogden, Steven. *Love Upside Down: Life, Love and the Subversive Jesus*. Winchester, UK: O Books, 2011.

———. *The Presence of God in the World: A Contribution to Postmodern Christology Based on the Theologies of Paul Tillich and Karl Rahner*. European University Studies, Series XXIII: Theology. Bern: Peter Lang, 2007.

O'Murchu, Diarmuid. *Adult Faith: Growing Wisdom and Understanding*. New York, NY: Orbis, 2010.

Packer, James I. "The Centrality of Holy Scripture in Anglicanism".
Pp. 29–47 in *The Future Shape of Anglican Ministry*. Ed.
Donald M. Lewis. Vancouver, Canada: Regent College, 2004.

Patterson, Stephen J. *The God of Jesus: The Historical Jesus and the Search
for Meaning*. Harrisburg, PA: Trinity International Press, 1998.

Peirce, Charles S. "Some Consequences of Four Incapacities". Pp.
156–89 in *Collected Papers of Charles Sanders Peirce 5*. Ed.
Charles Hartshorne and Paul Weiss. Rev. ed. Cambridge, MA:
Harvard University Press, 1960.

Percy, Martyn. *Shaping the Church: The Promise of Implicit Theology*.
Surrey, UK: Ashgate, 2010.

———. *Engaging with Contemporary Culture: Christianity, Theology
and Concrete Church*. Surrey, UK: Ashgate, 2005.

Pickard, Stephen. *Called to Minister: Vocational Discernment in the
Contemporary Church*. Canberra: Barton Books, 2009.

———. "Theological Education: An Anglican Way of Wisdom". Pp.
43–52 in *Facing the Future: Bishops Imagine a Different Church*.
Ed. Stephen Hale and Andrew Curnow. Melbourne: Acorn,
2009.

———. *Theological Foundations for Collaborative Ministry*. Surrey,
UK: Ashgate, 2009.

Plant, Stephen, and David Horrell. "Same Song-Sheet: Different
Tunes? Biblical Scholarship and Systematic Theology on
Reading the Bible". *Epworth Review* 30,2 (2003): 42–49.

Porter, Muriel. *Sydney Anglicans and the Threat to World Anglicanism:
The Sydney Experiment*. Surrey, UK: Ashgate, 2011.

Postman, Neil. *Amusing Ourselves to Death: Public Discourse in the
Age of Show Business*. New York, NY: Viking Penguin, 1985.

Rahner, K. *Foundations of Christian Faith: An Introduction to the
Idea of Christianity*. New York, NY: Crossroad, 1976, 1978.

———. "Remarks on the Importance of the History of Jesus for
Catholic Dogmatics". Pp. 201–12 in *Theological Investigations
13*. London: Darton, Longman and Todd, 1975.

———. "The Position of Christology in the Church between
Exegesis and Dogmatics". Pp. 185–284 in *Theological
Investigations 11*. London: Darton, Longman and Todd, 1974.

Reventlow, Henning Graf. *History of Biblical Interpretation*. 4 vols. Atlanta, GA: Society of Biblical Literature, 2009.

Robinson, Roy. *The Thoughtful Guide to the Bible*. Alresford, UK: O-Books, 2004.

Rorty, Richard. *Contingency, Irony and Solidarity*. Cambridge, UK: Cambridge University Press, 1989.

———. *Philosophy and The Mirror Of Nature*. Princeton, NJ: Princeton University Press, 1979.

Rowland, Christopher and Jonathan Roberts. *The Bible for Sinners: Interpretation in the Present Time*. Adelaide: ATF Press, 2008.

Rurlander, Daniel. "The Bible in the Academy and the Church". *Reformed Theological Review* 61,3 (2002): 148–59.

Salmon, James and Farina, John, eds. *The Legacy of Pierre Teilhard de Chardin*. New York, NJ: Paulist Press, 2011.

Schneiders, Sandra M. *The Revelatory Text: Interpreting the New Testament as Sacred Scripture*. San Francisco, CA: Harper, 1991.

Schüssler Fiorenza, Elisabeth. "Reading Scripture in the Context of Empire". Pp. 157–71 in *The Bible in the Public Square: Reading the Signs of the Time*. Ed. Cynthia Briggs Kittredge, Ellen Bradshaw Aitken, and Jonathan A. Draper. Minneapolis, MN: Fortress Press, 2008.

———. "Jesus of Nazareth in historical research". Pp. 29–48 in *Thinking of Christ: Proclamation, Explanation, Meaning*. Ed. T. Wiley. New York, NY/London: Continuum, 2003.

———. *But She Said: Feminist Practices of Biblical Interpretation*. Boston, MA: Beacon Press, 1992.

Schweitzer. Albert. *The Quest of the Historical Jesus: A Critical Study of its Progress from Reimarus to Wrede*. New York, NY: Macmillan Publishing Company, 1968 (original ed. 1906).

Scott, Joan W. "After History?" *History and the Limits of Interpretation: A Symposium*. Draft: Rice University, February 20, 1996.

Shea, Victor and William Whitla, eds. *Essays and Reviews: The 1860 Text and its Reading*. Charlottesville, VA: University of Virginia Press, 2000 (original ed. 1860).

Silf, Margaret. *Roots and Wings: The Human Journey from a Speck of Stardust to a Spark of God*. Cambridge, UK: Eerdmans, 2006.

Slee, Nicola. "Word". Pp. 36–61 in *Journey: Renewing the Eucharist 1*. Ed. Stephen Burns. Norwich: Canterbury Press, 2008.

Smart, James, D. *The Strange Silence of the Bible in the Churches: A Study in Hermeneutics*. Philadelphia, PA: Westminster Press, 1970.

Smith, Christian. *The Bible Made Impossible: Why Biblicism Is Not a Truly Evangelical Reading of Scripture*. Grand Rapids, MI: Brazos, 2011.

Smith, Elizabeth J. *Bearing Fruit in Due Season: Feminist Hermeneutics and the Bible in Worship*. Minneapolis, MN: The Liturgical Press, 1999.

Sölle, Dorothee. *Theology for Skeptics*. Minneapolis, MN; Fortress Press, 1995.

———. *Thinking about God: An Introduction to Theology*. London: SCM Press, 1990.

Spong, John Shelby. *Re-Claiming the Bible for a Non-Religious World*. San Francisco, CA: HarperOne, 2011.

———. *The Sins of Scripture: Exposing the Bible's Texts of Hate to Reveal the God of Love*. San Francisco, CA: HarperSanFrancisco, 2005.

———. *Rescuing the Bible from Fundamentalism: A Bishop Rethinks the Meaning of Scripture*. San Francisco, CA: HarperOne, 1992.

Stephens, John and Robyn McCallum. *Retelling Stories, Framing Culture: Traditional Story and Metanarratives in Children's Literature*. Children's Literature and Culture. Oxford: Routledge, 1998.

Teilhard de Chardin, Pierre. *The Phenomenon of Man*. Perennial Modern Classics. New York, NY: Harper, 2008.

———. *The Future of Man*. Garden City, NY: Image, 2004.

Thiessen, Gerd and Annette Merz, *The Historical Jesus: A Comprehensive Guide*. London: SCM Press, 1998.

Tillich, Paul. *The Dynamics of Faith*. New York, NY: Harper and Row, 1957.

———. *Systematic Theology*. Vol. 1. London: SCM Press, 1951.

Trible, Phyllis. *Texts of Terror: Literary-Feminist Readings of Biblical Narratives*. Overtures to Biblical Theology 13. Minneapolis, MN: Fortress Press, 1984.

Verhoeven, Paul. *Jesus of Nazareth*. New York, NY: Seven Stories Press, 2010.

Westphal, Merold. *Whose Community? Which Interpretation? Philosophical Hermeneutics for the Church*. Grand Rapids, MI: Baker Academic, 2009.

Williams, Rowan. *Dostoevsky: Language, Faith and Fiction*. Waco, TX: Baylor University Press, 2008.

———. *On Christian Theology*. Oxford: Blackwell, 2000.

Scripture Index

Subject Index

Abraham, 16, 84
Allegory, 109
Anglican Church of Australia, x, 3, 19–23
Anglican Communion, x, 20, 22, 89–91, 111n
Anthropomorphism, 65
Apocrypha, 77n
Apocryphal Gospels, 108
Apophatic tradition, 64
Archbishop of Canterbury, 105, 107, 114
Articles of Religion, 10, 21, 86–87, 89, 90, 92n,
Authority (of Bible), ix, 1, 3, 9, 10–11, 20–22, 30–34, 44, 45, 88, 89,
Baptism, 36, 68, 93n, 102
Biblical Criticism, x, xi, 1, 2, 3, 4, 5, 12, 13, 23, 45, 83, 85, 87, 88, 102, 104, 105, 107, 108, 119, 122, 124, 126
Book of Common Prayer, 81, 84
Canon, 9, 10, 19, 20, 21, 22, 84, 103
Christology, 40, 41, 47, 67, 70, 72,
Conservatives, 11, 47, 59n, 75, 77n,
Cross, 15, 37, 67, 73, 74
Daily Office, 83–84
David, 13, 14, 66
Easter, 85
Enlightenment, ix, xi, 11, 55, 105, 109, 116, 117, 119, 120, 121, 125
Epistemology, 4, 29, 44, 45, 47, 51, 52–54, 56, 59, 86
Eucharist, 106
Experience, ix, 4, 9, 26, 28, 31, 32, 45, 47, 50–54, 56–59, 61n, 69, 71, 72, 74–75, 83, 87, 98, 108, 123, 125
Exegesis, 34, 47
Form Criticism, 30
Fundamentalists, 3, 4, 45, 54–55, 59n, 64, 75, 104, 121
Gender, x, 16, 65
God, ix, xi, 1, 2, 3, 4, 7, 9, 13, 15, 16, 17, 18, 19, 20, 21, 22, 23, 26, 27, 28, 31–32, 34, 35–39, 41n, 43, 47, 51–52, 58, 59n, 63–77, 81, 83, 87,

91, 93n, 96, 97, 98, 104, 105, 106, 107, 113, 115–16, 117, 120, 122, 123, 125, 127
Gospel of Phillip, 108
Gospel of Thomas, 108
Grace, 3, 4, 26, 34, 36, 127
Hermeneutics, 34, 45, 56, 57
Historical Criticism, 46
Historical Jesus, 4, 44, 46, 55, 58, 59, 70, 71, 77, 78n, 98
History, 13–14, 18, 45–46, 47–50, 55–56, 58, 60n, 71, 72, 105, 108, 113, 114, 115, 117, 119, 120
Hope, 2, 41n, 43, 65, 81, 84, 97, 111n, 127
Incarnation, 18, 25, 32, 44, 52, 59, 67, 77, 126,
Identity, 4, 20, 85, 87–91, 97–98, 118
Inerrancy, 11, 30, 35, 66
Inspiration, x, 18, 20, 21, 22, 23, 26, 32, 42n
Interpretation, 3, 4, 8, 12, 18, 29, 30, 32, 34, 40, 41, 44, 45, 48, 50, 54, 56, 57, 59, 70, 71, 90, 96, 104, 109, 115
Jesus, 3, 4, 14, 15, 16, 18, 22, 35–40, 44, 46–47, 51, 55, 57–58, 59, 63–77, 81, 90, 97, 98, 100, 101, 102, 104, 107, 110n, 116, 126
Justice, 19, 87, 88, 110, 115, 126
Lectio divina, 83
Lectionary, 4, 84, 90. 99–103,
Liberals, 11, 77n,
Literary Criticism, ix, 30
Liturgy, 59, 95–110
Love, 2, 28, 74–75, 115, 125, 126, 127
Mary and Martha, 38, 99, 108
Meaning, xi, 11, 15–16, 18, 22, 25, 26, 28, 29, 30, 31, 33, 34, 39, 40, 44, 57, 66, 85, 91, 101, 102, 103, 106, 109, 110, 113–26
Miriam, 84
Moses, 14, 84
Ordinal, 22
Peace, xi, 37, 88, 89
Positivism, 46

143

CPSIA information can be obtained at www.ICGtesting.com
Printed in the USA
BVOW010312080313

315012BV00006B/16/P